Jesus 101

straightforward answers
to
basic questions
about
Christianity

Leigh Scheele

Jesus 101 – straightforward answers to basic questions about Christianity
ISBN 1-930285-15-9

Copyright © 2003 by Leigh Scheele
Cover Artwork by Daphne Malone Hewett
Published by The Master Design
    in cooperation with Master Design Ministries
PO Box 17865
Memphis, TN 38187-0865
bookinfo@masterdesign.org
www.masterdesign.org

Unless otherwise noted, Scripture quotations are from the KING JAMES VERSION as translated in 1611.

Scripture quotations marked NIV are taken from the HOLY BIBLE, NEW INTERNATIONAL VERSION © 1973, 1978, 1985 by the International Bible Society, used by permission of Zondervan Publishing House. All rights reserved.

Printed in the USA by Bethany Press International.

JJ

Contents

Chapter Five
<u>Does faith make a difference?</u> 65

Topics of Discussion:
What is faith?
Jesus' teachings on faith
What Jesus taught about the lack of faith
How to achieve greater faith
Faith: the ultimate stress buster!
Guard your heart
Have faith in the will of God

Chapter Six
<u>Is God still answering prayer?</u> 81

Topics of Discussion:
When it seems that prayers aren't being answered
Is it okay to ask Him more than once?
How God uses our prayers of faith
"Praying-through" in intercession
What are the basic essentials of personal prayer?
Praying in the name of Jesus
Waiting on God
Using the Lord's Prayer as a guide
Prayers of agreement
Prayer and Fasting
Praise and Worship
Final Thoughts on Prayer

Dedications

To my father, John, who, after becoming saved at the age of 87, went on to be with the Lord as this book was being prepared for publication.

To my mother and stepfather, Maryestel and Bill, whom God used to cheer me on in this effort and who give so selflessly of everything they possess!

To my daughters, Nicole and Brooke, who are still in shock over the changes which God has wrought in their mother!

Preface

"My people perish for lack of knowledge"
Hosea 4:6

I thank God for directing me to absorb the instruction and guidance of a number of anointed Bible teachers, who have presented foundational truths to me over the past years. But it was the Holy Spirit who *taught* these truths to me…giving me discernment on certain issues, and further illumination and revelation on others.

Before calling me to set my life apart for Him, God used me as a teacher in a variety of secular settings. I was labeled a "teacher's teacher," but I was a totally "clueless" Christian!

I sought after every kind of information and knowledge, accumulated degrees and licenses, and considered myself to be conversant in a wide variety of topics. Regarding my alleged faith, however, I had more questions than answers. I actually assumed there *were* no answers…Christianity seemed to be shrouded in mystery and embraced by many people whom I considered to be terribly naive! I eventually allowed myself – like many other seekers of "the truth" – to be lured into New Age philosophies, where I remained for many years, with one foot still in the liberal Christian church.

After a long series of life and health crises, I finally told God that I was willing to try it *His* way (whatever that might be)…which resulted in an experience similar to being strapped into a motorcycle sidecar, and being told to "hold on"! God proceeded to take me careening through a three-year crash course in being born again, Spirit-filled, sitting under anointed teaching, devouring the Bible, and forsaking all of my worldly ambitions and interests, in order to know Him intimately, and serve Him exclusively.

The Holy Spirit began to teach me the answers to all of my questions about Christianity which had gone so long unanswered. I had one "Eureka!" experience after another and, ultimately, He started sending people to me who needed the same type of information… all culminating in God *compelling* me to write this manuscript!

There are masses of people all over the world who are hungry for the "truth"— starving to know more of the things of God! So, if you are a non-Christian, a "New-Ager," a new Christian (or a curious, or confused, or timid, or defeated, or weak, or quasi Christian), you are welcome to share in this abbreviated synopsis of what I have received from God!

Please grab a Bible of any translation, and take the time to read, with an open heart, the Scriptures which are quoted and referenced. Invite God to speak to you through them, Spirit to spirit…even if you have never opened a Bible before. (Don't allow the Scripture from Hosea, quoted above, to paint your self-portrait!)

I pray that if your mind has been struggling with any of the questions addressed in this book, that the answers which I have received will provide a foundation for the Holy Spirit to teach *you* that which He would have you to understand. Not my truth—but *His*!

May God bless you richly for seeking Him, and may some small piece of this writing help you come to realize the joys of *oneness* with the Lord!

Leigh Scheele

"Whom say ye that I am?"

(Matthew 16:14–16)

Chapter One
What is the truth about Jesus?

This question may or may not reflect the cry of your heart or your most burning issue with Christianity, but without it, the rest is moot! The truth is, most inhabitants of this planet just don't "get it" about Jesus!

The majority of the secular world acknowledges that such a person existed, taught and ministered to the masses, and was crucified on a cross at Calvary, flanked by common thieves. But history doesn't give us any revelation about who He *really* was.

Christians believe that He was born to a virgin and that He was raised from the dead. So, is it simply because of these *miracles*, that the world celebrates Christmas and Easter? We know that He is referred to as the Son of God, but aren't we *all* sons of God? What sets Him apart? We hear that He is the Christ, the Messiah (Anointed One), and that He is called Emmanuel ("God with us"), but what does that mean?

Who exactly is He? This discussion will endeavor to pull together enough meaningful threads of (seldom taught) Bible-based revelations, to weave a tapestry of Jesus in your heart and mind—something substantial enough to wrap your faith around!

If you are thinking, "What makes you think that I would believe what the Bible says?" then I am 99% certain that you have never given God a chance to speak to you *through* it! This is your chance to painlessly expand your information base, and then ask the Holy Spirit to confirm or deny what has been presented to you.

The seemingly larger-than-life description found in the word Emmanuel ("God with us") might be the perfect place to begin examining Jesus' identity, because the existence of the Spirit—the true person—of Jesus did not begin in Mary's womb, nor in the stable in Bethlehem.

We can't fully explain the deity of Jesus without referencing the Trinity, so the first part of this discussion will attempt to briefly encapsulate the essence of God as a triune being and lay the foundation for Jesus' incarnation. Then we will examine the dual (God/man) nature of His life and its meaning to mankind. We will also consider some of the stumbling blocks to belief and talk about who Jesus is *not*!

We must never think that we have "arrived" at understanding the complexity of the Trinity or at knowing all there is to know about God. For one thing, it would be presumptuous, because He is so vast and we are so constrained by our physical senses…but it is also impossible because He has no intention of revealing all of Himself before we see Him face to face (1 Corinthians 13:12; Isaiah 55:9).

Most Christians do not question the *deity* of Jesus or the Holy Spirit. The major stumbling block is that we don't fully understand the mechanics and logistics required for one being to have multiple parts of Himself existing in different places, yet still be just one being. But, He is *God*. Most of His abilities are unimaginable to our human minds!

Jesus is part of the Trinity, but not part of the mystery. His divine origin and His divine existence at this moment are clearly documented in Scripture, as we will note.

In seeking revelation on how to explain His role in the Trinity, it helped me to remember that the whole is the sum total of its parts. I only began to grasp the magnitude of who God *is* when I studied, individually, the parts of the Godhead—Father, Son, and Holy Spirit—then put them back together as one.

Likewise, I learned, after feeling for years that there was something I was "missing" about Jesus, that I had to break it down. He was fully God, yet fully man. It helped when I examined His humanness apart from His deity (and the origin of each) then reassembled Him!

God as a Triune Being

God is one God in three persons. The Bible doesn't actually use the word "Trinity," but "Godhead" (Colossians 2:9; Romans 2:20). The Godhead has always (for eons before the birth of Jesus) consisted of God the Father, God the Word, and God the Holy Spirit.

Please realize that Christians didn't invent the concept of the Trinity to fit their beliefs. The Bible states very clearly: "For there are three that bear record in heaven, the Father, the Word, and the Holy Ghost; and these three are one" (1 John 5:7).

It is a difficult concept for some. It might help, however, to consider that we humans also have three distinct components: spirit, soul and body...all in one person.

(Some people mistakenly assume that the spirit and soul are the same entity, but your spirit is that part of you that is made in God's image, and your soul is your human mind, emotions and personality. When you are saved, your spirit begins to receive enlightenment (John 15:26;16:13), but your soul (which must be regenerated) resists receiving the truth. The Bible refers to men's souls as being "afflicted," "weary," "lustful," "sorrowful," "destroyed," etc...but, none of these adjectives are applicable to your spirit! The Bible tells us that the Word of God divides and separates the spirit from the soul. (Hebrews 4:12). Both the spirit and the soul are eternal. After you leave this life, you will continue to live *somewhere* – based on certain choices you made – for all eternity. See Matthew 10:28;25:46 and Mark 8:36-39.)

The point to remember at this moment is that we have three elements to our existence, and God has three elements to His. Originally known as Father, Word, and Holy Spirit...now most commonly referred to as Father, *Son* and Holy Spirit. But, we're getting ahead of ourselves!

When He made man (Genesis 1:26), God said, "Let US make man in OUR image, after OUR likeness," yet in Genesis 1:27, He reverted back to the singular pronoun, ("So God created man in HIS own image")...illustrating that the singular *and* plural pronouns are interchangeable in reference to God! He repeated this plural reference in the account of the Tower of Babel (Genesis 11:1-9) in stating, "WE will come down and confuse their language."

Most of us have no trouble grasping the concept of God the Father…we pray to Him and make reference to Him regularly. I have always loved God, and I can remember believing that it would be disrespectful to my Father in heaven, to give "equal billing" to any other part of the Trinity. This constraint blocked me for years from receiving a fuller revelation of who *God is*, and from sincerely opening my heart to Jesus and the Holy Spirit.

In Genesis 1, you will notice that "God created" many things…the heavens, the earth, the firmament, the creatures, the sun, the moon, and man; yet, most of those things were *spoken* first by God the Word. There are even elements of creation which the Bible describes as being simply *spoken* into existence (not made or created)…"Let there be light….Let the waters be gathered to one place, and the dry land called earth….Let the earth bring forth grass and seed." Even the creatures, after they were created, were commanded to "procreate in their kind" by the person of God called "The Word."

Please retain this image of God the Word *speaking* things into existence. We will revisit Him more fully when we discuss Jesus, below.

God the Holy Spirit

As for the Holy Spirit, He didn't reside *in* men on earth in Old Testament times. He was sent to us by Jesus, when Jesus returned to heaven (John 16:7;15:26). The Holy Spirit is inextricably linked to Jesus (John 7:39). Nonbelievers may have any number of other, ungodly, "spirits" residing in or interacting with them, but not the

Holy Spirit of God (1 John 4:1-3)! He comes to dwell in us when we invite Christ into our lives (Luke 12:12; John 14:15-17), and He always testifies of Jesus (John 16:14).

Genesis 1:2 says, "The spirit of God moved across the face of the waters." Nothing ever happens until the Holy Spirit moves! The entire Bible was dictated and written by Holy Ghost dictation. God caused Mary to become impregnated by His Spirit. One is drawn to Christianity by the Spirit of God; and Jesus will be revealed to you by the Holy Spirit. Unless God the Father appears to you in a pillar of fire, or Jesus comes down off His throne before His second coming, then your interactions with God and Jesus are occurring primarily through the Holy Spirit. However, He receives very little recognition in most denominations!

In many Christian churches, the Apostles' Creed is recited every Sunday. The third part of that creed (after honoring God the Father and Jesus) sates, "I believe in the Holy Spirit, the Lord and giver of life, *who proceeds from the Father and the Son, Who with the Father and Son is worshipped and glorified"* Yet, often, the existence of the Holy Spirit isn't acknowledged in their sermons, their worship or in their lives.

Jesus says in the Bible that the *only "unforgivable* sin" is to blaspheme the Holy Spirit (but that blasphemy of Himself *is* forgivable – see Matthew 12:31). The Bible also admonishes us, "Grieve not the Holy Spirit" (Ephesians 4:30), and "Quench not the Spirit" (1 Thessalonians 5:19). Most denominations, however, seem to be *dis*interested in tapping into the blessings of the presence of the Holy Spirit here on earth. (A growing number of individual ministers and non-denominational churches embrace Him, of course, and these churches are experiencing exponential growth worldwide – see Acts 2:17-21.)

Just as I often use the term "God" when I am referring to Jesus, I also will say, "God said," when speaking of hearing a personal word through the Holy Spirit, because He, too, *is* God. You can distinguish them, but you can't separate them!

If you would like to experience the Holy Spirit more fully in your life, then you are encouraged to take God up on His promise in Luke 11:11:

> "If you know how to give good gifts unto your children: how much more shall your heavenly Father give the Holy Spirit to them that ask Him?"

Understanding Who Jesus Is

The Bible actually gives us concrete specifics about who Jesus is. If He has been presented to you in ambiguous terms, or as a figure whose persona has been "hyped" by overzealous believers, then please balance the scales (of your heart and mind) with the following pre-sentation of a few facts from God's Word, then ask God to show you which side carries the weight of truth!

If you grasped the previously mentioned concept of God the Word, then understanding who Jesus is will be a lot simpler for you. The Scripture that spells it out for us most clearly is John 1. (A portion is quoted here, but it is suggested that you read the entire gospel of John as your starting point in the Bible, followed by the other three Gospels.)

"In the beginning was the Word, and the Word was with God, and the Word was God. He was with God in the beginning. Through Him all things were made, without Him nothing was made that has been made. In Him was life, and that life was the light of men. The light shines in the darkness, but the darkness has not understood it...(10) He was in the world, and though the world was made through Him, the world did not recognize Him. He came to that which was His own, but His own did not receive Him. Yet to all who received Him, to those who believed in His name, He gave the right to become children of God. (14) The Word became flesh and made his dwelling among us. We have seen His glory, the glory of the One and Only, who came from the Father, full of grace and truth." (John 1:1-14, NIV)

If you didn't thoroughly digest that passage, please go back and meditate on it some more...it is essential to grasping the full meaning of Christianity (also see Philippians 2:6-11). Any Christian who isn't comfortable freely using the name of Jesus simply doesn't have a revelation of who He is or what the Bible teaches...Old and New Testaments: **Jesus is God the Word, made flesh. Fully man. Fully God.**

Let's break it down:

His Humanness

God created, and the Holy Spirit placed, what must have been a divine-origin sperm into the womb of a teenage Jewish virgin named Mary. (I choose to use the word sperm, rather than fetus, because the Bible tells us that the Messiah would come from "the seed of a woman," which means Mary's egg had to be involved. This also fulfills the requirement of being in the blood line of Abraham, Isaac and Jacob, and David.) Mary was betrothed (a one year waiting period before consummated marriage) to a Jew named Joseph. The resulting baby's fleshly body, and the body of the man He grew to be, was fully human. The Bible tells us that He was subject to the same temptations as every mortal man, yet sinned not.

The Bible repeatedly refers to Jesus as the "only begotten Son of God," yet because of His mortal mother, His mortal ancestry, and because of God intentionally allowing Him to experience the human side of life, so as to become a model for us...He often referred to Himself as the "Son of Man."

Just as in our own lives, everything meaningful in the Son of Man's life was subject to the timing of God the Father. God moved Jesus into His ministry at the age of 30, and Jesus waited for His "time" to come – God's time for revealing the fullness of Jesus' identity and purpose. When He performed His first miracle at the wedding in Canaan, Jesus chastised His mother for suggesting to the host that He could solve the problem of having run out of wine. "My time is not yet come." Yet, He unceremoniously proceeded to turn the water into wine, and His ministry of miracles was begun (John 2:4).

For the next three and a half years, Jesus did exactly what God said to do, and said exactly what God said to say (John 7:16; 5:30), but as the day of His physical death was drawing nigh...He did the *most human* thing of his life. Kneeling in the garden of Gethsemane, sweating blood at the realization of what His sinless human body was about to have to endure (all the sins of the world), He asked God to reconsider this plan (Mark 14:36; Matthew 26:39).

(If I were He, I would have been hoping this would turn out to be an Abraham-like experience…that God would provide an alternate sacrifice at the last minute, once I had proved my willingness to obey Him!) But immediately, Jesus remembered His faith in, and obedience to, His Father…and the commitment which His spirit had made before the incarnation, and He said, "Not My will, but Thine, be done." He carried out the rest of the plan in dignity and near-silence, although He could have destroyed His enemies with one word. (Even the soldiers who came to take Him captive fell backward to the ground when He identified Himself to them! See John 18:6 and 10:18.)

What a magnificent gift to us, that God had this Gethsemane moment of Jesus' human weakness recorded in the Bible! It comforts me to see that this man, begotten of God, with the spirit of God the Word residing inside Him, truly *does* understand our weaknesses!

It is so important that we realize that Jesus didn't just go through the motions of humanness, protected by God from fleshly emotions and fears. He wasn't supernaturally spared from suffering, just so that God could symbolically say that the price was paid for our sins. God truly did *sacrifice* the only Child for whom He was the sole biological father. He not only turned His back on His Son and let Him suffer ("Why hast Thou forsaken Me?" Mark 15:34), God actually caused the sins and diseases of the entire world to attack Jesus' body as He died (2 Corinthians 5:21).

With the words "It is finished," the monumental part of this task was completed. An opportunity beyond imagination had just been afforded to any human who would ever live: The opportunity to step outside of "the law of sin and death" and into a new covenant with God…totally forgiven, saved for eternity, and viewed through the filter of the righteousness of Christ. All available for the choosing…because of God's grace, and mercy, and love…and at a great personal sacrifice to God Himself (John 3:16).

His Deity

You and I are spirit beings, with a soul, living in a body. And our spirit is an image of God, residing inside of us. However, there is one major spiritual difference between us and Jesus!

God created us, but God did not provide the male *seed* for our procreation. Each of us was begotten by an earthly, human, biological father. Dogs beget dogs, fish beget fish, elephants beget elephants, man begets man, and *God begets God*.

Jesus did *not* have an earthly father. Mary was a virgin, singled out by God for her faithfulness to Him. According to Luke 1:26-38, He sent the angel Gabriel to reveal His plan to her, so that she might prepare her heart for the miracle which was about to take place in her body. Jesus' biological father was God Almighty, Creator of heaven and earth. Thus, Jesus is His **only begotten** Son!

Jesus Himself instructed His disciples, "All power is given unto Me in heaven and in earth. Go ye therefore, and teach all nations, baptizing in the name of the Father, and of the Son, and of the Holy Ghost" (Matthew 28:19). (That verse alone should

11

dispel any argument that "Jesus didn't claim to be Deity.")

In addition to having divine physical genealogy (the biological son of God), Jesus – as we learned from the previous verses from John 1 – was, in His Spirit, *God the Word* (also see John 10:30). This means that He gave up all the honor and glory and majesty of reigning in heaven, to come to earth as a lowly human, and to become the blood sacrifice for a world of thankless sinners. It means that He gave all of mankind the opportunity (the choice) of wiping the slate clean, and starting afresh with God.

What was the significance of a **blood** sacrifice? Any medical doctor can tell you that "life is in the blood." Blood is probably the most precious commodity on earth—more valuable than silver or gold. It can only be manufactured in the bone marrow of our bodies. God designed it, with its own micro-universe functioning within its cells, to carry and sustain life on this planet. He has good reason to value it as the ultimate creative miracle. We (who have the most to gain from it) are the ones who have given blood a gruesome connotation!

God had established as law that "the wages of sin is death" (Romans 6:23). In the Old Testament, He allowed men to substitute the blood of a perfect, first-born animal, such as a lamb, in exchange for giving up their own life as a result of their sin. This was His foreshadowing of the day when He would offer the perfect (sinless) first-born "lamb of God" as a sacrifice for the sins of the whole world.

When Jesus said, "It is finished" (John 19:30) and died on the cross, it looked to the world as though "The End" should be flash-

12

ing across the screen of His life story. But, as we know, it was just the beginning!

We worship a risen, living Lord—the living Word.

I am ever mindful of what Jesus did for me, yet, when I talk to Him and think of Him, I am not speaking to a broken body on a cross. I see Him alive and victorious, returned to His royal position of power and glory. Remember, Jesus' tomb is *empty*! He didn't arrive in heaven as the spirit of a man who had died. After His death, He was resurrected back to life on earth (including His body, which ate and drank…yet was glorified, transfigured from a mortal body into an immortal body), and then ascended – not as a spirit, but still in human form, (in front of witnesses) – into heaven, after 40 days of being seen by scores of people.

God the Word now reigns again in heaven, in the ascended body of the man called Jesus Christ. True Christian believers understand that Jesus is *God the Son*!

Who Jesus is not!

Many nonbelievers acknowledge Jesus as being a great prophet of God. This is especially true in these days of interest in Islam and Buddhism – the theory that Jesus was one of several great teachers, like Mohammed and Buddha.

"New-Agers" have described Him in a myriad of ways – one quote, which I will paraphrase here, says: "Christ acts as mediator between our personality and our soul…His mission on earth was to teach us how to obtain harmony and communion with our higher self, and thereby obtain perfection…thus also taught the lord Buddha and other great masters...how to obtain perfection." If you think this sounds "reasonable," you are deceived!

Yes, Jesus was the only perfect man, and we are to imitate Him, but He didn't come so that we can be "perfect" and in "harmony with our soul." He came so that we might have eternal life (rather than the punishment which we deserve), and that we might be free of the bondage of the enemy. Jesus came to become the mediator between *God and man* (1 Timothy 2:5). He came to become the sacrifice offering – the scapegoat – for man's disobedience and sinful nature. This planet would have been "toast" a thousand times over, and all life snuffed out thousands of years ago, if man had been required to pay the price for his own sins!

I agree with C.S. Lewis, the author of *Mere Christianity*, who emphasizes the fact that either *everything* Jesus said about Himself is true (such as: "I am the way, the truth and the life." "No man comes to the Father but by Me." "If you deny Me before man, I will deny you before My Father." "I am the Bread of life, he that comes to Me shall never hunger." "He that believes on Me has everlasting life." "He that has seen Me has seen the Father," "I am the door, by Me if any man enter in, he shall be saved"; "I that speak to you am He [the Messiah]"), or He was a complete madman and liar, not worthy of our respect at any level!

Allow me to take this a step further and suggest to you that either Jesus is exactly who He claims to be (as God the Father gave Him the words to speak, revealing progressively more truths about Himself toward the end of His ministry), or the world has been deceived. This would mean that all the Bibles, churches and de-

14

nominations – as well as the calendar system by which we measure our years – have been built on a gargantuan hoax and may as well be destroyed!

You may believe or not believe the Bible, that's your freewill choice. But, I implore you: Don't demote Jesus to merely being a great teacher and prophet of God. That's not one of the options… choose again! He was either a lunatic or *is* the Savior of the world!

Why was all of this necessary?
Why do I need a Savior?

God sees the end from the beginning, and always knew that men would become so decadent that He would either have to destroy the world (again) or provide an alternate plan. The "new plan," of course, had been in place forever and was prophesied over 300 times in the Old Testament! (One of the more obvious prophecies is Isaiah 53.)

The new plan was to provide a Savior for all of mankind, who would offer us an alternative to experiencing God's eventual wrath for rejecting and disobeying Him. Accepting the conditions which God was offering wasn't intended to be an obvious, easy choice. It was intended to separate the wheat from the chaff, the sheep from the goats (see Matthew 25:32-33). It was intended to separate those who hear His voice and who obey His word from those who prefer to go their own way – to their own proud destruction. And it was intended to require the exercise of faith, with no tangible or visible guarantees of success…just the promises of God.

Man seemed incapable of living in righteousness on his own, so

God would impute that righteousness to those who accept His Son, and then empower them to take control over their own flesh, through His residing in them. (True, not *all* Christians choose to exercise this power!)

Prior to Jesus' birth and death, the world operated under the law of sin and death: You sin…you pay dearly for it, or offer a sacrifice for it. Those who believe in the only begotten Son of God operate under the New Covenant of sanctification and justification: You are seen by God through the filter of His Son, and your sins were paid for at the Cross. This sounds like a "deal" that is too good to be true, but God promises it over and over again in the New Testament (Romans 3:24;4:25;5:1,18; Acts 13:39; Galatians 3:24) as well as in the Old Testament. Isaiah 53:5 says, "He was wounded for our transgressions."

The Bible tells us that Jesus is sitting at the right hand of the Father, and that He will come again, in glory, (not as a lowly servant/teacher/prophet again), to judge both the living and the dead, and that His kingdom will have no end (Matthew 24).

One reason God has appointed Jesus to be our judge is that He is the only member of the Godhead who knows what it is like to be human. (He also knows that when He, by the presence of the Spirit of God, is living inside of you, it *is* possible to resist evil and the lusts of the flesh!)

Forever is a long time, my friend. Please think for a moment about the worst day of your life…when you felt the farthest from God. Then remember a moment (however fleeting) when you experienced His presence or His blessing. Reflect on which experience you would want to dwell in for eternity, because, according to Jesus, it will be one or the other (Mark 16:15)! There are those who might consider me gullible for believing the Bible, but if *I* am wrong, then I will have lost nothing. If *they* are wrong, they lose everything... forever. Please pray for wisdom and discernment!

Stumbling blocks to belief

"My heart says, 'Yes,' but my mind says, 'No'"

I can well remember some of the stumbling blocks to receiving these truths.

- "How logical is the virgin birth?"

- "The miracles can't be true! What about the laws of gravity and weight and mass...surely He didn't really just ascend up into the atmosphere!"

- "What about all of the people who are of other faith systems, or have never heard about Jesus?"

- "Well, maybe these things resonate in my spirit as being true, but I don't have the certainty that many Christians seem to have."

If I may address these concerns, in order:

Regarding the virgin birth: As you study the Old and New Testaments, one thing that might impress you is how God always chose weak, ordinary people to be His especially anointed servants. (He still does, by the way!) The weaknesses, lusts, disobedience and failures of such servants as Moses, Abraham, David, Jesus' disciples and the Apostle Paul are all documented, as well as their sins...large and small. There are no "Barbie and Ken" dolls in the Bible, and there is no whitewashing of their characters! It was also the *sinners*

17

to whom Jesus *un*apologetically devoted His time and attention during His ministry.

So, I ask you: WHY would God reveal all the disgusting truths about His chosen people, but fabricate a lie about Mary's virtue? "God is not a man, that He should lie" (Numbers 23:19). The world could have accepted a Messiah who was fully mortal, yet highly anointed of God (as a matter of fact, that's what non-believing Jews are looking for today)—but, God had a better idea!

Regarding the ascension (and other miracles): It might help to spend some time in those Scriptures where God reminds us of *who* He is, of what all He has done, and of what He is able to do (Job 38 and 39, for example).

Also, keep in mind: The same God who created and maintains the delicate balance of keeping the earth precisely the right distance from the sun (so that we neither burn up nor freeze)…and who keeps it rotating on its axis at exactly the speed necessary to have uniform days and nights…and revolving around the sun *while* rotating (so that we can experience seasons)…and who maintains just the appropriate amount of gravity to keep us loosely anchored to the earth as it is hurtling through space, yet not so much gravity that birds and planes can't fly around in our atmosphere…*that* God (I would propose to you) can suspend any force He has created. He can suspend it for one individual (as He did for Elijah and Jesus), or for the masses (as the Bible describes He will for the believing Body of Christ (see 1 Thessalonians 2:1;4:16,17; Matthew 24:21-44)).

The promise that we will be changed, "in the twinkling of an eye," from mortal into immortal bodies (1 Corinthians 15:52,53) means that we will receive glorified bodies, as Jesus did…molecularly reconstructed. *That* should facilitate levitation, considerably!

If that idea just seems too far-fetched to you, you're not alone! But, don't let it pull you off-track on your journey with God. Many good Christians can't imagine the actual fulfillment of the prophecy of the "gathering up" of the Church and some differ as to whether it will occur before, during, or after the 7 years of tribulation. We will all find out together some day! God doesn't often break His own spiritual or physical laws, but He has reserved that right. *"I will have mercy on whom I will have mercy, and I will have compassion on whom I will have compassion"* (Romans 9:15, also see Revelation 7:13-17).

Regarding followers of other religions: The short answer is that the "Good News" (the Gospel of Jesus Christ), which Jesus first disseminated to the Jews, then commanded to be spread to every living creature (See Mark 16:15; John 10:15,16), has been slowly covering the globe for 2000 years. In these last days, it is spreading like wildfire, through modern technology and worldwide evangelism, to the most remote corners of the earth.

God says that, to Him, *"A day is as a thousand years, and a thousand years is as a day"* (2 Peter 3:8). (That's two "days" gone by, now, and we all know what happened on the morning of the third day…Jesus came back!) God has always allowed other religions to exist, and has allowed mankind to choose whom they will serve, and how they will live…they just don't get to choose the *consequences* of their choices (see Deuteronomy 30). God knows that before He sends the Messiah again, He will have provided a way for

19

all nations to hear the Truth, and either accept or reject it.

I am not God, and I can't speak for Him on anything that He hasn't dictated to be written into His Word. I *do* know that there is only one way to be *certain* of spending eternity with Him in heaven. Another faith system may have given you something to "hope" for or ways to "work" your way into heaven, but according to the New Testament, that is not how heaven operates! (See Galatians 2:16, Ephesians 2:8,9; Titus 3:5.) Only Jesus gives you *certainty* in your heart, and has done all the work of salvation for you. Just rest in Him and have faith in the promises of God for those who receive His Son (John 25-30)!

[Mind you, "faith without works is dead," also (James 2:26). But this means that ONE way to exhibit our faith, is through acting it out...and, yes this *will* manifest certain blessings and rewards...but it's not by our works that we are *saved* from eternal separation from God, it is simply by belief in Jesus. It is possible to be "blessed," yet not saved!]

There is only one Savior...only One who can transform your life, bring peace to your heart, and set you squarely in the center of God's will for your life; only One who can assure your eternal future, and who willingly became the sacrificial lamb for your sins; only One who is God incarnate; only One who says "I am the way, the truth, and the life. No man comes to the Father but by Me" (John 14:6).

What does *your* "guru," or "prophet," or "teacher" promise you? And what authority backs it up? Where is his body at this moment...dead in a grave? I think I'll stick with the Savior who sits at the right hand of the Father, and to whom *every* knee will bow!

Regarding lack of certainty and faith: The human mind is not capable of conjuring up the kind of faith required to reach certainty about the unseen. The good news is that we don't have to "pump ourselves up"! The Holy Spirit will supernaturally impart divine faith *to* us, after we have accepted Jesus as Savior. This faith is increased as we continue to walk with the Lord and to seek God through His Word.

I assure you, the faith that is leaping off of this page is not of my doing. I *do* exercise it regularly, however, and God keeps rewarding it and giving me more! I see miracles now on a regular basis, because I have the faith to believe for them and the power of the Holy Spirit is alive in me.

Believe it or not (in spite of my enthusiasm!), the purpose of this book is *not* to lure, or draw you into becoming a Christian. It's not even possible for me to do that...that is God's job. "No man can come to Me, except the Father which sent Me draw him" (John 6:44). The purpose of this book is to obediently (in my personal walk with God) share information, which has the ability to set you free.

If you are being drawn by the Spirit of God, you will know it, although the devil *will* try to talk you out of it! (Oh yes, I forgot to mention...there definitely *is* a ruler over the spiritual powers of darkness.) That's for a later discussion, though (see Chapter 3).

The bottom line regarding "Who Jesus Is," is this: Are you being urged in your heart to say, "Jesus, *if* these things about You are true, then I want to know You! Please come into my life and reveal

Yourself to me"? If so, you have nothing to lose…except possibly your pride, which is the one sentiment which God despises above all things (Proverbs 6:16)!

NOTE: A personal invitation (as in the above illustration) is essential. Jesus will stand outside your door until the day you die – unable to help you – because the Father has instructed Him: "Only go in where you're invited" (see Revelation 3:20). The Holy Spirit will stir up the realization of a need, or possibly a yearning, in your heart, but then you must act on it. God insists on making it a free-will choice.

If you are someone who believes that everyone goes to heaven, and that a loving God wouldn't judge His children so harshly as to condemn them to eternal separation from Him, then you are entitled to cling fervently to that belief, until the day you stand before Him! But, please, be aware that you have created a God who fits *your* desires and expectations, rather than loving the Creator who has revealed Himself to us for thousands of years through the revered, divinely-inspired writings known as the Holy Bible.

The God of the Bible (who is still revealing Himself today) has given His creation certain instructions which require their awareness, and has presented them certain choices…only one of which will result in His eternal protection and provision. Many people are attracted to the promises of Christianity, but don't like the way that God packaged those promises! In his book entitled *Great Divorce*, C.S. Lewis predicts that, in the end, there will be just two groups of people: those who say to God, "Thy will be done," and those to whom *God* will say, "Thy will be done."

"I have set before you life and death,
blessing and cursing. Choose <u>life</u>"
(Deuteronomy 30:19)

"I am come so that they may have <u>life</u>..."
(John 10:10)

"I am the resurrection and the <u>life</u>"
(John 11:25)

"Ask and ye shall receive"
(John 16:24)

Chapter Two

What is Christianity? Who is a Christian?

I certainly don't presume to be the ultimate authority, or judge, of who is or is not a Christian, and I apologize in advance for any toes that this chapter may step on!

But as a teacher who has promised to provide "straightforward answers," I would be remiss to exclude the evidence in the Bible which suggests that God *did* have an ideal in mind, when He drafted the master plan (which we call Christianity) for making peace with mankind. It would be irresponsible of me to ignore Jesus' statement that there will be 'followers' of His to whom He will have to say, "Depart from Me...I never knew you" (Luke 13:27).

I would consider this writing a failure if even *one* reader received such a rebuke from the Lord based on ignorance – especially after a lifetime of thinking that they were in pretty good shape spiritually! So, may I proceed?

First, let's deal with how Christianity is perceived by the world, and by many people who call themselves Christians: Most people would answer that Christianity is a religion. It may appear to be a multifaceted, multi-denominational, multi-creed religion that an onlooker could assume is open to any *number* of interpretations, since there seems to be a virtual smorgasbord of doctrines.

The true answer, however (and the only explanation of which I can imagine God wholeheartedly approving), should, probably, be drawn from the lives of the early followers of Christ, and from the orders Jesus gave to His disciples when He appeared to them after His resurrection: "Go ye into all the world, and preach the gospel to every creature. He that believeth and is baptized shall be saved; but he that believeth not shall be damned" (Mark 16:15). Pretty strong words, huh? Well, Jesus tended to "tell it like it is"!

We could simplify the discussion of this topic, and have it begin and end with one sentence: "If you believe in Jesus, confess that belief, repent, and are baptized... then you are saved, and you are a Christian." If that settles it for you, then, bless you! Perhaps you are already operating in the center of His will for your life and/or you don't feel particularly called at this moment to examine Christian growth and maturity. If anyone wishes to dig a little deeper, however, please read on!

Would you agree that a faith system built around this (or any other) person should be based on the "informed consent" of its followers? If so, then claimants of Christianity should have at least an *assenting* heart-knowledge of who Jesus is and what He truly stands for. (Likewise, those who say, "Thanks, but no thanks," should *reject* Him from an informed perspective!) The preceding discussion, on understanding Jesus and the Trinity, attempted to provide foundational Bible-based truths about Jesus' identity – a realization of which is imperative to comprehending Christianity!

The name "Christian" actually means "little Christ" or "little anointed one." It was used to describe the followers of Jesus, who were commanded to spread the gospel, to receive the Holy Spirit, and to do, through His power, the same things that Jesus did when He was among them. I would suggest to you that this is still a viable, objective definition of what God has equipped willing, obedient Christians to become…"little Christs." Not perfect humans, but perfectly committed to allowing Him to do His work, through their lives. "I can do all things through Christ who strengthens me" (Philippians 4:13). "As He is so are we in this world" (1 John 4:17).

If that thought seems overwhelming to you, remember…it says "God has equipped" those who are "willing." This is not a challenge, which we set our minds to accomplish! To *try* (in our flesh) to be Christ-like, would be futile, unattainable, and prideful. The Bible says: "Not by power, nor by might, but by My Spirit, saith the Lord" (Zechariah 4:6). God never calls us to do anything that He doesn't provide, by His Spirit, the means with which to accomplish it!

The degree to which any Christian reflects Christ-likeness results from the degree to which one has allowed God to have His way in their life – the degree to which they have used their freewill choice, to yield themselves to God the Father, God the Son, and God the Holy Spirit—and to His Word. *Not as a mindless puppet,* but through the voluntary act of saying to God, "I choose to reject all human and spiritual influences which would draw me away from

Your perfect will for my life. As Jesus did, I *choose* to put my focus on obedience to You."

Does every Christian attain this? Obviously not!

Does every Christian desire to attain this? Sadly, no.

Why not? Partially, because many Christians don't understand that such godliness is available to them and, partially, because many people interpret "meeting the minimal requirements for salvation" (knowing that you are forgiven, and going to heaven when you die) as being *all there is* to being a Christian.

Why would they think that? Possibly, for one (or all) of the following reasons:

- Perhaps they have never been taught what God has to say about His expectations for us. (i.e. they have never read the Bible)
- Perhaps they have never realized *who* they are in Christ (have never taken into their hearts Jesus' revelations of all that is imparted to and through us, by belief in Him)
- Perhaps they have never allowed the Holy Spirit to ignite their faith and empower their Christian walk "You will receive power after the Holy Ghost is come upon you" (Acts 1:8, also see 1 Corinthians 2:9-14).
- Perhaps they routinely allow the devil to fill them with spiritual apathy, failing to use our one and only *offensive* weapon against his lies "Take…the sword of the Spirit, which is the Word of God" (See Ephesians 6:10-18).

Aren't those premises a bit outdated? Many among us are (wishfully) assuming that God has mellowed out over the past 2000 years.

We are hoping that He has succumbed to society's norms and that, therefore, the Bible no longer reflects His current thinking. I would invite you to prayerfully consider the following Scriptures: Malachi 3:6; Matthew 5:18; Luke 16:17; 1 Peter 1:23-25.

Be careful not to misinterpret God's love, grace, mercy, and forgiveness as weakness – as His having lowered His expectations for His children. If your logic tells you that 2000 years is too lengthy a time for God to still be expecting conformance to a set of "antiquated" spiritual laws, then please try to consider it from this perspective: 2000 (plus) years is a *generously long* time for Him to have waited patiently for a world of spiritual rebels to begin accepting the plan (complete with instructions) which He has continued for centuries to offer them. This is the very plan through which we came to *experience* the precise love, grace, mercy, and forgiveness which we take for granted!

A Personal Perspective

Admittedly, we believers don't spend a lot of time trying to formulate a (even subjective) definition of Christianity. Neither had I before the Lord compelled me to begin this writing. As soon as the question was posed to my spirit, however, the following affirmations came flooding through me, almost instantly! If you are a Christian, perhaps your spirit will attest to similar convictions.

Christianity, to me, is a belief system which is evidenced in my life in the following manners (with suggested supporting Scriptures):

It is embracing the person that Father God gave to the human race as a peace offering. (2 Corinthians 5:18; Colossians 1:20; Ephesians 2:14; John 3:16; Romans 5:8)

It is believing that Jesus *is* all that He said He is. (Matthew 10:39-40;13:41-43; Mark 10:29-30: John 3:15-18;5:24;6:35,47; 10:10,11;14:6)

It is allowing Jesus to change my heart and life, knowing that He will help me to become as much of what God created me to be as I am willing to become. (2 Corinthians 5:17; Romans 12:2)

It is sending an R.S.V.P. to God's hand-delivered invitation to have my name added to the Lamb's Book of Life. (Membership benefits include living eternally in God's presence and being escorted there the moment my life on earth ends) (John 10:27-29; Revelation 21:24-27)

It is honoring a plan that only a God of miracles could have designed and implemented for saving the world, while remaining true to His pre-established commandments. (A blood sacrifice for the remission of sins) (Matthew 26:26-28; Mark 14:24; John 10:11; Acts 20:28; Romans 5:9)

It is being a thankful recipient of God's best idea, His greatest sacrifice and His most generous blessing, to a mankind which deserved to be destroyed for sin and disobedience. (Titus 3:3-7; Mark 10:45)

It is being unashamed to speak the truths which God reveals to me – through His Word, His Spirit, and His presence in my life – about His only begotten Son. (Luke 9:26; Matthew 10:33)

In other words, embracing Jesus has totally transformed my life and He is still perfecting in me: belief, faith, peace, love, joy, gratitude, surrender, obedience, humility and boldness…all to the glory of God!

Christian Humility

If the terms "humility" and "boldness" seem contradictory, it is because we are accustomed to the world's definitions. God included much teaching on humility in both the Old and New Testaments. In Jeremiah 9:23,24, He told us not to glory or boast in wisdom, might, or riches, but said, "let him who boasts boast about this: that he understands and knows Me, that I am the LORD, who exercises kindness, justice and righteousness on earth, for in these I delight." (NIV)

Meekness and humility are not to be confused with weakness. Any disciple of Christ can tell you that Christianity is not for sissies! Jesus humbled Himself to come to earth and become a servant of man. He was bold and confident about His Father's will, and about the mission which He had undertaken. Yet, on the night before His crucifixion, He began to wash His disciples feet, in a demonstration of His commitment to the virtue of humility. He left them with a visual and spiritual lesson that we are never to feel superior to another, but that we are to be a servant of all, in obedience to God's Word.

We are to humble ourselves before God, in the knowledge of the following truths: that all of our gifts come from Him, that He "opposes the proud and exalts the humble" (Matthew 23:12), and that *He* will promote us "in due time" (1 Peter 5:6). But from this humble position, we are to imitate the Apostle Paul, who asked the Ephesians to pray for him, "that whenever I open my mouth, words may be given to me so that I will fearlessly make known the mystery of the gospel...Pray that I may declare it fearlessly as I should" (Ephesians 6:19,20).

Is everyone a Christian who claims to be?

Personal experience has taught me that people refer to themselves as being "a Christian" for many different reasons, and from a number of different perspectives! At one point or another in my life, I have fallen into almost every one of the following categories, and you could probably add others – so please don't feel there is condemnation or judgment in this list! Reviewing some of my former positions in faith reveals to me, however, that many years were spent believing that I was a Christian, before I truly *was*.

One might respond "yes" to the question "Are you a Christian?" for any one (or combination) of the following reasons:

1. By default. ("Well, I'm not a Buddhist, or a Muslim, or an atheist, so I guess I'm a Christian.")
2. Because of having been baptized as an infant, or having been raised in a Christian family, though never having personally invited Jesus into their life.
3. As someone who believes in, and seeks God, but who thinks Jesus was primarily a great prophet (and who possibly thinks that those who claim to know and love Him are somewhat naive or irrational).
4. As a "closet Christian," who *hopes* "this thing I've prayed about Jesus" is true, but who sees religion as a divisive subject. "Everyone should keep their beliefs to themselves." No one knows whether they are a believer or not.
5. As someone who truly believes "who Jesus is" and "confesses" their belief and is probably headed for heaven when they die, but whose daily life doesn't at all reflect a Christian walk. Per-

haps they are as defeated, judgmental, and depressed as the rest of the world.

6. As someone who strives to live a "good Christian life" and to "do good works," but doesn't believe in the truth or relevancy of the Bible and has no real relationship with God.

7. As someone who once walked with the Lord, but who backslid and is living in some manner of sin or bondage.

8. As a charismatic, who is captivated by the idea of the power of the Holy Spirit, yet not grounded in the Word.

9. As a Christian who is Word-filled, Holy Spirit-filled, enjoying intimacy with all three persons of the Godhead (Father, Son, and Holy Spirit), witnessing as the Holy Spirit leads and is actively involved in a church where they receive anointed instruction in the Word of God.

10. Some combination of the above!

There could be many variations on this theme, but if you personally relate to numbers 1 through 4, perhaps you would consider praying for revelation regarding what you *truly* believe versus what Jesus calls us to do and believe. If you relate to numbers 5 through 8, you might consider spending more time in the Word and/or ask to be empowered by the Holy Spirit!

You may be a devout Christian who doesn't fit neatly into any of the above categories. If you sense, however, that "Christian #9" above is portrayed as the "ideal"…well, according to the Bible, that would be the case! Assuming that this person has a loving and obedient heart toward God, and a loving and forgiving heart toward man, then the Christian walk, as described in #9, reflects much of the totality of what God calls us in His Word to be.

The good news is that this "ideal" is attainable and sustainable. It doesn't call for us to be "perfect," mind you, but to attempt to be emptied of our former selves, and filled with every good thing He has to offer us – which would include: His love, His grace, His Son, His presence, His Word, His wisdom, His guidance, His protection, His blessings, and—yes—His Spirit and His power! (See Acts 1:8)

His grace and love are ours through no effort, whether we deserve them or not. The other things require some degree of our participation. Some are ours for the choosing, some are ours for the seeking, and some are ours for the asking.

To be really thorough, one should *choose* and *ask* and *seek* each and every one of them! *He* is already seeking *you*, or you would never have opened a book with this title.

This discussion is not meant to suggest that all Christians should be cookie-cutter-identical in their preferred manner of worship. God left us just enough gray areas in Scripture to ensure that the Church would be multifaceted…not to mention the extremely different natures He imparted to us as humans! A cursory glance around our planet will reveal how much God loves diversity. In spite of our innate differences, however, we (the Church) are called to be one body, and of one *mind*, as Jesus and the Father are one (1 Corinthians 1:10). One of God's universal laws is that there is power in unity, but the Body of Christ has a bit of a way to go before achieving it!

Why is there so much division in the Church?

Some of the division found in the Church is merely doctrinal interpretation, which may never be resolved until Jesus comes. Much of the confusion surrounding Christianity today, however, is compounded by the fact that there are a number of denominations whose appointed electorates have chosen to make the church more "seeker-friendly." This has often been translated into watering down God's Word, to make it more acceptable to man – rather than calling for man to conform his behavior to being more acceptable to God.

Perhaps these churches haven't read what Jesus had to say to the Seven Churches, throughout the second and third chapters of Revelation! Jesus commends each church on what is pleasing to Him, but then takes issue with them on the where they've "missed the mark" ("I have somewhat against thee."). He gets more to the point of His true feelings, in Revelation 3:15-16: "I wish thou wert cold or hot. So then because thou art lukewarm, and neither cold nor hot, I will spew thee out of My mouth."

Have you ever taken a sip of a beverage that you expected to be hot, only to feel room-temperature "muck" in your mouth, so that you just spit it out? Well, I believe that Jesus' frustration here stems from the fact that He has been appointed to judge us. He knows exactly what He is going to do with the "cold" (throw it out), and He has eternal blessings in store for the "hot" – but those are the only two verdicts available!

What we see happening in the Church right now, as the cold get colder and the hot get hotter, is that those who are straddling the divide (which is becoming deeper and wider) are going to be torn asunder and fall into the abyss…so they might as well go ahead and jump to one side or the other! Matthew 24:12 tells us that Jesus said, "Because of the increase of wickedness, the love of most will grow cold, but he who stands firm to the end will be saved."

If you find yourself thinking, "Well, Christianity is so restrictive!", I would answer that I prefer to describe it as having parameters and as being "capable of definition"… and that the definition would have to, at minimal, include belief in who Jesus said He is, and a desire to follow His teachings, and keep His New Testament commandments.

These include: "Love the LORD thy God with all thy heart and all thy soul and all thy mind,… and love thy neighbor as thyself. On these two commandments hang all the law and the prophets" (Matthew 22:37-40).

[In other words (for those who say that we only need to know the New Testament), the Ten Commandments, which were taught in the Old Testament, can be covered by strict obedience to these two laws. This new commandment does *not* negate the commandments of the Old Testament, it merely *consolidates* them! Jesus very deliberately said, in Matthew 5:17-19 (NIV): "Do not think that I have come to abolish the Law or the Prophets; I have not come to abolish them, but to fulfill them. I tell you the truth, until heaven and earth disappear, not the smallest letter, not the least stroke of a pen, will by any means disappear from the Law until everything is accomplished. Anyone who breaks one of the least of these commandments and teaches others to do the same will be called least in the kingdom of heaven, but whoever practices and teaches these commandments will be called great in the kingdom of heaven."]

Now, mind you, we Christians obey the Commandments out of love and appreciation for God – because of the unmerited grace He has shed on our lives. We are not obedient out of fear of damnation (we are forgiven), nor out of a desire to be "pious" ("holier than thou"), but out of a desire to *please* Him. This is true "fear" of the Lord!

Devout Christian believers with a heart for God are not totally sinless, but they are supernaturally attributed with righteousness (Romans 3:21-22; 2 Corinthians 5:21), and are imparted a conviction for attempting to stay in obedience to Him.

However, merely living a "good," or even "godly" life, and obeying the commandments, doesn't necessarily mean that you're a Christian—although they may make you a good person. (Good Jews and Muslims and Buddhists might do those, too!)

The Bottom Line

The purpose of this entire discussion, of course, has been to illustrate that one is not a Christian simply because they embrace Judeo/Christian principles. One, also, does not automatically become a Christian by going to church regularly and *exposing* themselves to the faith.

Christianity is *not* a "philosophy" based on the teachings of Jesus, nor is it a design-your-own-belief-system. However, until one is experiencing firsthand what it *is*, it can be difficult to discern "what is wrong with this picture?".

36

What frequently is *missing*, is the lack of *true* belief in the namesake of the faith system! We can easily pass ourselves off as Christians to the world, but God sees our hearts and knows our thoughts. The Bible says that God will not be mocked (see Galatians 6:7).

The cure for lack of belief? "Draw nigh unto God and God will draw nigh unto you" (James 4:8). Do you want a "sure thing"? Ask Jesus to come into your heart and to prove the following Scripture to you in a meaningful way:

"For the preaching of the cross is to them that perish foolishness; but unto us which are saved, it is the power of God"
(1 Corinthians 1:18)

Chapter Three

Do Powers of Darkness Really Exist?

I don't want to spend an inordinate amount of time on this subject, because the solution is far more important than the problem. But it is the beginning of spiritual discernment to understand that NOT everything in the spirit world is of God!

High school mass murderers, international terrorists, sex and drugs in elementary schools (but no prayer or Ten Commandments!), partial birth abortions, pornography and pedophiles, ethnic cleansing, child abuse, spousal abuse...the list of evidence that there is a sinister influence which preys on the human mind is convincing. Such things are certainly not of God, but are emanating from the same larger spiritual realm. Those of us who are in the visible realm comprise only a portion of the number of spirit beings which are in existence! The Bible assures us that there are angels (several kinds, actually) and mentions the devil (and devils) 169 times. A major focus of Jesus' healing ministry was the casting out of demons, and setting the "captives" free.

The ruler of darkness is as real as God is real, but his days are numbered! (See Revelation 20:2,3,10,14.) The Bible tells us that the spiritual entity who came to be known as the devil named Satan, was originally an angel named Lucifer, who wanted to be exalted above God, and was, ultimately, cast out of heaven (see Isaiah 14:12). Jesus stated in Luke 10:18, "I beheld Satan as lightning, fall from heaven."

We are told in Ezekiel 28:14-17, that God had originally entrusted him with great gifts and great authority, but that he became filled with pride because of his beauty and wisdom. God threw him to the earth, and ultimately, he will be consumed with fire (Revelation 20:10).

In the meanwhile, however, the Bible warns us that we are to "be sober, be vigilant; because your adversary the devil, as a roaring lion, walketh about, seeking whom he may devour" (1 Peter 5:8). The word "may" connotes permission. Who is giving him permission to devour us? Primarily, WE ARE! God gave us free will to choose life or death, good or evil (Deuteronomy 30:15). When we reject the ways and words and will of God, then we are (whether by omission or by commission) choosing to follow the ways and words and will of the enemy, and opening up our lives, and the lives of our offspring, to his influence.

Wait a minute! That's not fair! Nobody ever told me that my actions would affect the lives of my children!

Under the New Covenant (which Jesus brought to the earth) our confessed sins are covered by Him, "who became sin for us, so that we might become the righteousness of God" (2 Corinthians 5:21). But anyone who is not operating under the protection of the New Covenant is still subject to the rules of the Old Covenant. In the Ten Commandments, God stated clearly the following: "I the LORD your God, am a jealous God, punishing the children for the sin of the fathers to the third and fourth generation of those who hate Me" (but now, for the good news!) "but showing love to a thousand generations, of those who love Me and keep My commandments" (Exodus 20:5,6).

Being punished for the sins of the fathers may seem harsh, but I sincerely believe that God set it up that way so that men (who perhaps don't value their *own* lives enough to resist sinful behavior) might have reason to consider the ramifications of their actions on the lives of their children and great-grandchildren.

Before you go grumbling to God about generational sins, please notice how much greater and long lasting the promise of blessing is than the promise of cursing! One thousand to four! If you give someone the privilege of choosing whether he is going to live in a manner which may inflict pain and suffering on four generations of his "seed", or in a manner which may result in blessings for a thousand generations of them, then that would seem to be adequate reason for one to be walking with God! What rational parent wouldn't consider that to be a pretty good incentive for getting his 'act' together?

God is a GOOD God! He has a deep, multifaceted, valid beyond our comprehension, purpose for everything that He does. He has our best interests in mind. He is *not* setting us up for failure, but giving us every possible tool and piece of information we need to live in total victory. "I wish above all things that you prosper and be in health, even as your soul prospers" (3 John 2). He is not schizophrenic...blessing one moment, and cursing the next. He is not the one who chose to have sin and evil in our lives, we are. But He *is* a God of order. There is divine *order* to all of nature, and there are consequences when it is disturbed. Even the physiological operation of our bodies is preprogrammed with *order*, and when we make poor health choices, we throw our systems out of balance and suffer illness. Obviously, there is need for law and *order* in the communities and countries where we live, and we pay the penalty when it is not upheld. God also foresaw the necessity for *spiritual law and order*, until such a time as the Prince of Peace would be reigning in all men's hearts.

Generational curses have existed in all of our bloodlines, and are still rampantly in operation in many of them, and are epidemic in countries which are still worshipping false gods. How can it be "Not Fair!" when we had the warning carved in stone, and carried down from Mount Sinai by Moses over 3000 years ago; then printed in every translation and edition of the Bible (the best-selling book of all recorded history – which is available in almost every language on earth, and found in every hotel room, and in most of our homes)? This is not an obscure footnote in the Bible, and it isn't New Testament gospel...it is in the *text* of the *Ten Commandments*, believed by God-fearing people for millennia to be the audibly dictated word of God!

God actually answered the Old Covenant cries of "unfair" through His prophet Ezekiel, in Chapter 18. He stated that those who live righteous, repentant lives, and who keep ALL His statutes would not die for the iniquity of their fathers. God further said that His ways *are* equal, and that He takes no pleasure in the death of those who refuse to live righteously.

Sadly, most people are only familiar with the condensed version of the Ten Commandments. The devil actually knows the Bible better than most Christians do (he quoted it to Jesus in the wilderness, in Matthew 4:6), which is why he can deceive us so easily! He is called "a liar and the father of lies" (John 8:44 NIV), and is an expert at speaking lies which are close enough to the truth, so that they have a credible "ring" to them. The battleground where the devil and his demons attack us is in the space between our ears—they place thoughts in our minds. Lucifer was a brilliant and creative angel, and is a cunningly manipulative devil! He knows and preys upon our weaknesses and can fill our minds with a myriad of excuses for doing the totally wrong thing.

I think the devil may have, to a large extent, given up on trying to talk people out of believing in "a god". He just doesn't want us to know Jesus, or The Word, or the Holy Spirit, because then we will learn how to recognize him, and learn of the power we have been given over him – how to defeat him!

The curses in my family's genealogy alone were staggering and blatantly obvious to anyone who can grasp the concept. The devil has a destructive plan for every person's life, just as God has a perfect plan for every life. There are people in my family who have suffered terribly for their spiritual ignorance. But, I have made the conscious decision that the buck stops here! I have repented before God for every ancestor back to Adam and Eve, for sins known and unknown, and for God to forgive us for our ignorance and disobedience. (This is Scriptural, see Nehemiah 9:2.) I am determined to restore my children and future grandchildren's spiritual DNA! From now on: "As for me and my house, we will serve the LORD" (Joshua 24:15)! That begins with the only life over whom I have any control—mine!

Are "New Age" Practices Demonic?

Let me answer that question by sharing three Scriptures with you. Please meditate on them, and direct your questions to God:

> Deuteronomy 18:10-12: "Let NO ONE be found among you...who practices divination, sorcery, interprets omens, engages in witchcraft, or casts spells, or who is a medium or spiritist or who consults the dead. Anyone who does these things is detestable to the LORD, and because of these detestable practices the LORD your God will drive out those nations before you."

> Isaiah 47:13,14: "Let now the astrologers, the star gazers, the monthly prognosticators, stand up, and save thee from these things that shall come upon thee. Behold, they shall be as stubble; the fire shall burn them; they shall not deliver themselves from the power of the flame: there shall not be a coal to warm at, nor fire to sit before it."

> Galatians 5:19-21: "The acts of the sinful nature are obvious: sexual immorality, impurity and debauchery; idolatry and witchcraft; hatred, discord, jealousy, fits of rage, selfish ambition, dissensions,

43

factions and envy; drunkenness, orgies, and the like.
I warn you, as I did before, that those who live like
this will not inherit the kingdom of God."

I shamefully admit that I spent many years involved in various New Age practices before I had the new birth experience. I thought, during that time, that the word "occultism" just referred to obviously evil things, such as black magic and voodoo-ism and devil worship. I considered myself to be a seeker of God and of truth. I wanted to know about (and be proficient in) every avenue which leads to information about the universe. I studied astrology and tarot cards, and consulted psychics when I was in desperate need of answers. I truly believed that God intended for us to discover and utilize these methods of tapping into *all* of His knowledge (which I assumed was only hidden from people who weren't inquisitive or industrious enough to find it!)

One of the first things I realized when I got into the Bible was that so many concepts (which I had thought were revolutionary and originating from "new age awareness") were not "unique" or original at all! Many "New Age catch phrases" are plagiarized straight from the Bible, then slightly twisted to make them sound original, and to make the *real* truth sound perverted. I assure you that God is still sovereign, and the world is not on autopilot, but He HAS established universal spiritual laws, or truths, which we, ourselves, call into operation by our words and actions.

For example, take the new age expression "You create your own reality" (which seems to leave God completely out of the equation). If you latch onto that phrase and put it into operation in your life, guess what? You, probably, will see positive results! WHY?? Because the Word of God says that "As a man thinks in his heart, so is he" (Proverbs 23:7), and Jesus says in Mark 11:23 that "If you believe that those things which you say will come to pass, then you will have what you say." These are two of the "universal truths" which GOD put into action! The Bible also says, in Matthew 5:45, that "The rain falls on the just and the unjust." This means that His laws, and the benefits of them, work in the lives of both believers and unbelievers! So, what appears to be an affirmation of the human ability to direct the universe is *actually* God the Word (Jesus), bringing His principles to fruition in your life!

Likewise, the world's prediction that "What goes around, comes around" is true, because of Biblical laws which state that "what you sow, so shall you reap" (Galatians 6:7) and "give and it shall be given unto you." It is not your "karma" which has determined your destiny. It is your beliefs and *choices* (or possibly those of your ancestors, if you are not under the cover of the New Covenant.)

Perhaps you have heard of people who have had "amazing" experiences with spiritualists. The reason that psychics and astrologers can see the future, is that the devil is telling them *his* plan for your life. Of course, they can tell you everything about your past, because the devil and his demons have *seen* it! Demons (being supernatural beings which are not bound by the laws of nature) can seem to perform miracles by taking away those illnesses which they have put on someone. But, don't confuse that with the miracles and healings of the Holy Spirit! Remember, we learned in the discussion on understanding Jesus and the Trinity that the Bible is very clear about the fact that the Holy Spirit is only available to believers in Christ (see page 6). Many people who consider themselves to be

45

"spiritual" and who refer to "spirit" manifesting things in their lives, are dancing with demons, unless that spirit comes through Jesus. And if that Spirit *does* come from Christ, the first thing He will do is point to Jesus, as being the Son of God and the Redeemer (John 14:26).

In these last days, God *is* dramatically "pouring out His Spirit upon all flesh" (Acts 2:17). He is raising up and anointing many more servants in the fivefold ministry within the Body of Christ ("apostles, prophets, evangelists, pastors and teachers" Ephesians 4:11-13). Great numbers of devout, born-again, Spirit-filled Christians are experiencing the miraculous these days. So if you are dabbling in New Age practices, please pray about renouncing them and then get hooked into the *winning* SUPER-natural team! (Hint: This fight is "fixed"! It may go the entire fifteen rounds, but the victor has already been determined!)

This will startle some of you (and anger others), but books and movies such as Harry Potter (which glorify and lure children into occult practices) are not any more "innocent" than books and movies which glorify and lead them into sex and drugs.

When I first found the three verses of Scripture relating to occultism (from Deuteronomy, Isaiah and Galatians), I was mortified to realize that I had been grieving the Holy Spirit for so many years. He proceeded to show me that, in the Garden of Eden, it wasn't the tree of good and evil, but the tree of the *knowledge* of good and evil, which they were forbidden to taste of. God was trying to protect man from even learning that evil existed, just as any good parent would prefer to spare her child from experiencing the things that nightmares are made of. We were not intended to know everything that God knows! But the devil was able to tempt Eve (who tempted Adam) into believing that God simply didn't want them to be as smart as He was. Mankind has been dealing with the devil (and with his own pride) ever since! "What good is it for a man to gain the whole world, yet forfeit his soul?" (Mark 8:36)

How do we overcome evil in our daily lives?

The road to victory begins with acquiring spiritual discernment.

The first place that God sent me, when He saw that I was *serious* about wanting my life to change and to be within His perfect will, was to a ministry which specializes in teaching about spiritual roots of illness and generational curses (Pleasant Valley Church in Thomaston, Georgia). There, I learned from Pastor Henry Wright the importance of spiritual discernment (knowing which things are and which are *not* of God).

Once we become familiar with God's ways and His desires for us, then it is possible to understand which parts of our own nature are obviously DIVINE in origin (are we loving, forgiving, generous, joyful, patient, peaceful, or humble?) and which parts are obviously NOT (are we untruthful, angry, prideful, impatient, addictive, abusive, AND/OR inquisitive of and inclined toward those practices, which are known to be abominations to God?).

Once we are armed with the revelation that our thoughts may not be our own, but that they can be influenced either for good or for evil, then we can begin to refuse to participate in those actions which are not of God. We can take control of our flesh, and say to the voices (lying spirits) in our minds: "The Lord rebuke you, Satan!" (Zechariah 3:2) "I will have no part of you, in Jesus' name!"

The most righteous person that you know frequently has unclean thoughts enter her mind—the difference is whether or not she speaks or acts from them. Controlling our actions begins with controlling our tongues. "Life and death are in the power of the tongue" (Proverbs 18:21. Also see Proverbs 12:18;15:4,17:27; James 3:5-10; Matthew 12:34 and 2 Timothy 2:23).

Don't fear the devil…that is just what he wants – to be exalted. Remember, he is a defeated foe, just desperately trying to take as many prisoners as he can before he gets thrown into the pit. He has no power over you that you don't give to him. Once you understand the ways in which you may be opening yourself up to his attacks, then you have the power, through the Holy Spirit, to stop it! The Bible says, "Submit to God, RESIST the devil, and he will flee from you" (James 4:7). Jesus said that He came to set the captives free (Luke 4:18) and that He has given us "power over all the power of the enemy" (Luke 10:19). But note that obeying God is a prerequisite to experiencing the power!

One excellent book designed to help you use Biblical principles to perform spiritual warfare through prayer is titled *Shattering Your Strongholds,* by Liberty Savard. It is based on the scriptural promise that: The Church has been given the keys to the kingdom of heaven, and that what we **bind** on earth is bound in heaven and what we **loose** on earth is loosed in heaven (Matthew 16:19). Entire congregations who have studied this book have reported being transformed by binding their minds to the mind of Christ, and their bodies, souls and spirits to the will and purposes of God. She also teaches how to bind the devil and loose his hold on everything he has stolen from us and our loved ones, and how to pray for lost children and for those in bondage.

If you feel that you are truly demon-possessed, as opposed to merely demon-oppressed (in your mind), or that you are a target of witchcraft, then I suggest you purchase a book such as *Deliverance from Evil Spirits* by Francis McNutt, or any work by Derek Prince. Ask God to lead you to a deliverance ministry which can help you. But do your spiritual homework first, or you will shortly be back in the same leaky boat!

Putting on the whole armor of God

By "homework", I mean that God has given us a checklist, which if we incorporate it into our daily lives, will work like preventive medicine against attacks of the enemy. It is referred to as putting on the "whole armor of God," as found in Ephesians 6:12-18:

> "For we wrestle not against flesh and blood, but against principalities, against powers, against the rulers of the darkness of this world, against spiritual wickedness in high places. Wherefore take unto you the whole armor of God, that ye may be able to withstand in the evil day, and having done all, to stand. Stand therefore, having your loins girt about with truth, and having on the breastplate of righteousness; And your feet shod with the preparation of the gospel of peace; Above all, taking the shield of faith, wherewith ye shall be able to quench all the fiery darts of the wicked. And take the helmet of salvation, and the sword of the Spirit, which is the word of God."

It is important to realize that this isn't merely a verbal checklist, but it requires that we *acquire* the qualities which comprise each piece of armor, which God then uses to form the spiritual protection. It isn't just the words, or the affirmation of the words, which protect us. We must also embrace and possess those attributes! The questions to ask ourselves are these:

Are my loins girded about with truth? I have learned that "loins" can refer both to our flesh and to our minds (see 1 Peter 1:13). So, we must make certain that our minds and the lusts of our flesh are "girded" (tightly contained, controlled) by the TRUTH, which is found in the Word of God.

Am I wearing the breastplate of righteousness? Am I in right standing with God, where my character and motives are concerned? If not, my heart and conscience are vulnerable to attacks of the enemy. "Out of the heart flows the issues of life" (Proverbs 4:20).

My feet being shod with the gospel of peace means this: **Am I walking in peace with my fellow man?** Do others see the reflection of the gospel in my behavior, where love and forgiveness are concerned? Am I easily offended? Do I walk the walk, or just talk the talk? (We aren't talking about self-condemnation here, but self-preservation. If we can get this thing right, the devil looses another inroad to our lives!)

Am I carrying the shield of faith? Do I keep this wall of faith positioned in front of me, so that when the devil shoots his fiery darts at me, they just bounce off? Or do I spiritually crumble at the least resistance? We are told to "walk by faith, and not by sight" (2 Corinthians 5:7). You may not yet see the results that you are expecting, but "they that wait upon the Lord shall renew their strength" (Isaiah 40:31). Keep that shield of faith up until God has either fulfilled His promise or given you a better plan!

Am I wearing the helmet of salvation? This one is a no-brainer—if you're not saved, then your mind is demon-bait! I have heard it said, however, that where the full armor of God is concerned, most Christians are *only* wearing the helmet of salvation, and the rest of their spiritual body is naked! They will certainly be going to heaven when they die, but they allow the devil to make their lives miserable until then, because of lack of knowledge or lack of interest in doing what it takes to protect themselves. We will discuss the topic of salvation in Chapter Seven.

Am I carrying the only *offensive* weapon in the armor of God? "Take the sword of the Spirit, WHICH IS THE WORD OF GOD." How can words be the only things that we can use to come against the devil? All of the other pieces of armor were purely defensive…keeping the devil away…but this is the one we can attack him with! The Bible says that, "the word of God is sharper than any two-edged sword" (Hebrews 4:12). If it was sufficient for Jesus, when the devil was harassing Him in the wilderness, it must be sufficient for us! "It is written…", "It is written…", "It is written…". There is an answer in the Word for anything and everything the devil might throw at us!

I will share with you my first experience with the power of the Word, because it was so life-transforming. A number of years ago, I was suffering with neurological (seizure) complications from chemical and radiation toxicity. I hadn't slept in weeks. Every time I would begin to fall asleep, I would experience a stroke-type explosion in my brain, and would go into convulsions. I felt so close to death that I asked my Christian step-father to sit by my bed and read the Bible aloud as I was attempting to fall asleep, in case I were to die. To everyone's amazement, as long as the Bible was being read aloud, the convulsions stopped and I was able to sleep!

For many days, my family arranged for someone to come and read the Bible all night, so that I could sleep without a convulsion. I didn't realize until months later, that my New Age activities had been leaving me wide open to a curse against my life. It was after being taught about spiritual discernment, that I understood that the demons attached to that curse were fleeing in the face of God's Word! The sword of the Spirit *is* the Word of God!

God used that experience to grab my attention in a dramatic way – and I have walked with Him ever since. Not only am I forgiven and saved for all eternity, but I am walking in increasing blessings, rather than curses. My case was heard and overturned by the SUPREME Supreme Court! Why? Because I responded to His call to "Come out from among them and be ye separate" (2 Corinthians 6:17) and because I try to make certain every day that I am physically and spiritually protected by affirming and *becoming* every piece of weaponry which He has so generously afforded me.

Be spiritually diligent enough to get yourself fitted with the whole armor of God, and don't leave your bed in the morning without it!

Chapter Four

Why is it imperative that we forgive others?

God's position on forgiveness

Of the many positive gestures which are demonstrative of Christianity, why have I singled out forgiveness as meriting a discussion of its own? Because it is a common stumbling-block to achieving intimacy with God!

Most of us believe that we have a valid reason for failing to forgive someone, and according to the standards of the world, we may be right! We could undoubtedly win many a sympathetic ear to our injury or insult, who would heartily agree that we are entitled to remain indignant about it.

However, Jesus gave us several clear-cut instructions on this issue to impress upon us that God sees it differently. God seems to view forgiveness as a prime opportunity for us to demonstrate that we are willing to try it His way. And He gives us plenty of motivation to make that attempt! "For when you stand praying, forgive, if ye have aught against any, that your Father also which is in heaven may forgive you your trespasses. But if ye do not forgive, neither will your Father which is in heaven forgive your trespasses" (Mark 11:25,26). Also, see Matthew 18:21-35, where Jesus says that we must forgive our brother "seventy times seven" times. Ouch! That's 490 times, but what He really means is, "Don't keep a count of the insults that come against you. Forgive them all."

Even when we say the Lord's Prayer, we give God our permission to forgive us our trespasses "as" (in the same manner that) "we forgive those who trespass against us" (Matthew 6:12). That can be a sobering thought! How many of us can honestly say that we would like for God to forgive us only to the same degree that we have forgiven those who have harmed us?

[As our world seems to be moving perilously closer to catastrophic wars, we should probably note that God's laws for personal interaction are different from His civil laws. As you can see in the Bible, governments who are protecting their citizens from the evils of danger or oppression are not expected to walk in love with their enemy! It is our job as individuals to attempt to generate an atmosphere of peaceful coexistence with our neighbor, but it is the job of a godly government to disallow and punish (locally and globally) those who reject moral law, and who are bent on evil and destruction. (See Romans 13:3,4; Luke 14:31; Matthew 24:6,7.)]

Why is it so hard to forgive?

Perhaps forgiveness is difficult because of pride, or fear, or because of wounded emotions which are rooted in feelings of rejection. Pride is something which we have to crucify in ourselves. No one else can do it for us, and God *won't*!

54

Fear is overcome by beginning to know God as your daddy in heaven, and by believing that He can be trusted to protect you in every circumstance imaginable until such a time as He brings you to Himself.

Rejection, however, is probably the most destructive of all emotions. When we feel rejected (which often begins in childhood), we begin to believe lies about ourselves, because we weren't taught, or don't have a sense of, who we truly are. These wounded emotions become compounded as we go through life – with every insult having added fuel to the fire. The truth is, however, that only God knows who we *really* are and who He created us to be. Every other perception and every other opinion—even our own—is just an illusion. HE, also, is the only one who really knows the heart and wounds of the one who injured us. So when we wallow in emotional pain, we are really boxing with imaginary shadows and cooking in a stew of our own making. One reason that we are instructed, "Judge not, lest ye be judged" (Matthew 7:1), is that we simply don't have all the *facts*!

When God looks at us, He sees our sweet, divine natures – separated from the negative effects which the world has had on us. He forgives us readily, easily, and completely, when we ask Him. He also knows that He has sown that same capability into our Christian spirits—the ability to *choose* to see others as He sees them, separated from their sinful natures. We can't do it alone, but we can allow Him to do it, through us!

Unfortunately, we also receive plenty of spiritual encouragement to remain in *un*-forgiveness because spirits from the dark side *de-*

light in watching us dance to that tune. They are constantly whispering it to us, and we are constantly taking the bait! The devil knows that staying in hostility is a blatant act of disobedience to God, and that when we choose to ignore or refuse to be obedient to God's commandments, we are crossing over into the enemy's territory! It can impede our healing, our prosperity and our general well-being, by blocking the blessings that God has in store for us.

Let me suggest to you that you only have two adversaries. One is your own flesh, which the Lord can help you bring into submission. The other is your *real* enemy…but it is not the person who has harmed you! Your only true enemy is the spiritual adversary of us all, who is able to attach himself to undiscerning people's wounds, and talk them into harming others. Assuming you were really harmed (and not merely being overly-sensitive or overreactive), then the person who hurt you was simply being used as a puppet by the devil. If you realize this, it will be far easier to obey Jesus' instruction to: "love (those whom you consider to be) your enemies, bless them that curse you, do good to them that hate you, and pray for them which despitefully use you, and persecute you" (Matthew 5:44).

Try to understand that people who do hurtful things are simply trapped in their own bondage. "Father, forgive them, for they know not what they do" (Luke 23:34) reflects a universal truth! The world is comprised of so many lost souls who haven't a clue as to who they really are or where they fit into God's divine plan.

Knowing who we are in Christ can set us free from harboring whatever offense may be thrown our way. Once we feel secure in

God's love, we begin to understand what is meant by the verse, "if God be for us, who can be against us?" (Romans 8:31).

What does God really expect of us in the area of forgiveness?

Here are some observations which I have (sometimes painfully!) received about God's position on this subject:

1. Forgiveness happens in the heart. Forgiving in your heart does *not* mean that you must remain in a situation which places you in physical or psychological danger. You can forgive at a distance!

2. To God, forgiveness has little or nothing to do with the offense which you have experienced—no matter how deliberately hurtful or unspeakable it may have been. As far as *you* (the wounded party) are concerned, God isn't looking as closely at the nature of the offense against you, as He is your *response* to it. You can choose to position yourself for a blessing from God, or to block the blessings, as a result of your reaction to it.

3. God *does* see and takes mental note of the emotional and mental affliction which you have been dealt by the offense, and if you handle it properly, He will see that you are, eventually, rewarded and more than restored for your trouble!

4. But, if you choose cling to anger, bitterness, or feelings of rejection, then—aside from the spiritual ramifications—the resulting stress will cause a physiological weakening of your immune system and some sort of illness or disease will ultimately result. ("A merry heart doeth good like a medicine, but a broken

57

spirit drieth up the bones" Proverbs 17:22.)

5. The actual nature of the offense is recorded on the ledger of the person who has harmed you. God will either bring that person to repentance, or judge them for it. "To me belongeth vengeance and recompense; their foot shall slide in due time" (Deuteronomy 32:35).

6. What is recorded in *your* life story is either:

   a. You asked God to help you forgive your offender

   -or-

   b. You chose to remain in unforgiveness

7. Once you have made the conscious choice to be obedient and forgive (whether you feel like it or not), then God will supernaturally begin to place forgiveness in your heart, which your woundedness would have never allowed you to accomplish through your own effort. One day there will be peace, where once there was pain!

8. The commandment to "forgive" also applies to forgiving yourself! (As does the necessity of asking God to accomplish it for you!) "Love your neighbor as yourself" (Matthew 19:19, Mark 12:31) presupposes that you love yourself. So ask God to help you see yourself as He sees you – without all your hang-ups! If you still feel guilty after you have repented to God, then ask Him to help you to experience His mercy, grace, and love toward you, and to help you understand that your sins have been *forgotten*, as well as forgiven (1 John 1:9, Isaiah 43:25, Psalm 103:12)! If anyone reminds you of your past, tell them, "Those things happened to someone else!"

How do I manage to stay in forgiveness?

I have two favorite Scriptures to "stand on" (recall, repeat, meditate on, remind God of) at times when I am tempted to backslide in the area of unforgiveness. One is: *"All things work together for good to them that love God, to them who are the called according to His purpose"* (Romans 8:28). This means that *all* things, ALL THINGS, **ALL THINGS** …even the painful things …are going to be turned by God into something good, because I love Him and I have yielded myself to His purposes for my life.

The second is an Old Testament verse that reflects the same promise. It is a quote of Joseph, who, fourteen years after his brothers had conspired to kill him (and had thrown him into a pit, and sold him into slavery), ultimately ended up being second in command in all of Egypt, and living in Pharaoh's palace. Joseph then told his brothers, *"Ye thought evil against me, but God meant it unto good, to bring to pass as it is this day"* (Genesis 50:20). The NIV translation says it this way: *"You intended to harm me, but God intended it for good to accomplish what is now being done."* He forgave everyone who had oppressed him, and saw the fulfillment of God's promise for his life! God turned all of those miserable circumstances into stepping-stones to royalty and the preservation of the people of Israel.

Some of the most powerful Christian leaders in the Church today have been raised-up out of abject poverty and unspeakable abuse into positions of power and influence in the Body of Christ. Why? Because their painful (but forgiven) experiences have created irrefutable testimonies to the healing, restorative, and recreative abilities and desires of God to transform, and then *use*, a human life! God is in the business of taking people out of "pits," and positioning them for a blessing. Our part is to keep our eyes on His promises and our hearts on obedience…for however long it takes for Him to bring the promises to pass, in His perfect timing.

Forgiveness is a sacrifice that we offer to God – as is praying "for our enemies" and "for those who despitefully use us." We die to our need to hold onto the anger and pain, and give it to Him, in faith that He will take that test and someday make it a testimony!

I once heard Bishop T.D. Jakes pose a question on the subject of forgiveness, which stopped me in my tracks, and ended up posted on the door of my refrigerator: *Who are you SO angry with, that it is worth messing up how your story ends?*

What if I have trouble forgiving my parents?

Many of us have issues with the quality of how we were parented, and some of us have serious wounds as a result of being mistreated, or rejected, by a parent. The above teaching, however, *is* applicable to forgiving the (intentional, negligent, emotional or physical) abuses of our moms and dads. So let's focus, first, on the spiritual significance of pressing in to obedience in this matter!

Compliance with all of the Commandments is essential to being in God's perfect will. But He must have known that "Honor thy father and they mother" would be a challenge for many of us, because He attached some additional promises to being obedient to it! God actually "sweetened the pot"…as if He was saying, "I'm going to throw in some extra blessings as an incentive on this one."

He knows that if you learn to respect the authority of your parents—which isn't always going to be easy, considering the human condition—then, you will respect the authority of your bosses, your government leaders, and your God.

Of course, the flip side of the promised blessing would be a withheld blessing, for all those who do *not* make the effort. Then, there is both the loss of the blessing, and a curse. (For some people, the punishment of a "curse" is the *only* incentive which would carry enough weight to sway them away from behaving in a vindictive or abusive manner toward their parents!)

As Christians, we live under grace. How much more are these blessings available to us, when we *choose* to place our parents in the position of being honored? How much more defeated is the devil when he cannot get a toehold into our lives because we are sold-out on acquiring the mind of Christ and on being in God's perfect will?

So, what are the promises which are attached to this commandment? The first one is found within the text of the Ten Commandments, itself, "Honor your father and your mother so that you may live long in the land the LORD your God is giving you." (NIV) Also, Deuteronomy 5:16 says:, "Honor your father and your mother, as the LORD your God has commanded you, so that you may live long and that it may go well with you..."

In the New Testament, Ephesians 6:1-3 says, "Children, obey your parents in the Lord, for this is right. Honor your father and mother—which is the first commandment with a promise—that it may go well with you and that you may enjoy long life on the earth." There are other New Testament references to honoring parents, such as Matthew 15:4,6;19:19; Mark 7:10;10:19; and Luke 18:20. It is, obviously, a priority with God!

You can see that, without proper instruction in the Word of God, we would be ignorant of the fact that *He* has determined that the very length of our lives, and the quality of our lives, will be affected by whether or not we strictly obey this one commandment!

Let's not leave the above verse from Ephesians 6, without pointing out that it continues: "And fathers, do not provoke your children to anger, but bring them up in the discipline and instruction of the Lord." The Bible teaches that as children we are to obey our parents. The only time we are permitted to disobey authority of any kind, is when it contradicts the Word of God. We see in this verse that fathers are admonished to *not* provoke their children to wrath. But, perhaps your father did so provoke you (or worse). Parents are also instructed here to raise their children in the knowledge of God. But, let's face it, most parents don't!

So, what do we do when we have become adults who don't respect our parents, because of their failures, or weaknesses, or abuses of authority? God's answer is that we forgive them, pray for them, and treat them with respect for the office they hold. Remember—you are only responsible for willful obedience to *your* part of the commandment. Your parent will answer to God for his or her shortcomings.

If your parents are not Christians, and/or are still behaving like heathens, you don't have to agree with them. If you are an adult, you certainly don't have to spend all of your weekends with them. But "to honor" means to pay "merited respect." The point to remember is that, even though *you* may not believe that your parents deserve your respect, God has placed over them a covering that demands it! Above all, if they are not Christians, pray for their salvation—that *someone* will lead them to know the Lord before they die! Ask God whether He has given that assignment to you, or if He simply wants you to model the love of Christ to them.

What if I keep falling back into old behavior patterns when I am around them?

In attempting to comply with God's commandment on this, it may help you, for a while, to imagine a red neon sign, flashing on your parents' foreheads: "THIS IS A TEST! THIS IS A TEST!" every time you see, or speak with them! Be determined to pass this test, with a sincere heart for doing the honorable thing. Imagine that Jesus is standing right there, encouraging you to treat them like friends, and empowering you to succeed in it. In fact, He is right there, through the Holy Spirit, doing just that!

Try to realize that, as soon as you get to heaven, you will be able to see your parents just as God saw them every time they repented—innocent and justified by accepting the Redeemer. If they are not Christians, try considering all of the emotional and spiritual baggage that they have been carrying, their lack of spiritual discernment, and their lack of understanding of God's will. This should help you to understand that they probably did the best they could with the information which they had at the time. So, you might as well get on with the act of forgiving them NOW!

Forgiving now will not only spare everyone concerned additional years of heartache, but will enable you to experience the joy of *feeling* God's pleasure as you mirror Him to your parents, to your own children, and to the world! If your parents are no longer alive, then you can still forgive them and demonstrate that same forgiveness in your speech and actions, with respect for their memory.

The main thing to remember about forgiving others, is that God didn't make it optional.

FORGIVENESS?? JUST DO IT!

Chapter Five
Does faith make a difference?

"Without faith, it is impossible to please God."

The author of Hebrews (6:7), goes on to explain to us that whoever comes to God must **believe** *not only* that He exists, but that **He rewards those who diligently seek Him!** That sounds great, and most of us believe that God is capable of rewarding us, but how does one come to that point of believing that He *is* going to do these things that He has promised, not for someone else, but *for me?*

What really *is* faith, anyway? Is it simply belief in something that can't be proved by empirical evidence? Is it merely "mind over matter"? Is it just making a decision to hold on tenaciously to an illusion, hoping that it will come true? The Bible says that *"Faith is the substance of things hoped for, the evidence of things not seen"* (Hebrews 11:1). In other words, when you have good reason to believe (to know...that you know...that you know), that what you are waiting for **is going to come to pass**, then you already "possess" its substance. You have all the evidence you need to feel certain that it will happen. What gives you that kind of assurance? Knowing that a promise is *true*, beyond a shadow of a doubt.

If you are a person who has always been honest with me, and I know you to be consistently reliable in what you say you will do, then, if you tell me that you are going to do a specific thing, such as meet me for dinner, or help me with a project, as far as I'm concerned, it's done—you will do it!

When God called a pagan named Abram to go to a foreign land and promised (when he was 75 years old!) to give him a son with his barren wife Sarah, Abram's faith didn't waiver...even though he was almost 100 years old before God brought it to pass. Why did he not doubt? Because he **believed the one who had made the promise!**

Abraham (as he was later re-named by the LORD) also passed the ultimate **test** of faith, by not faltering when God later told him to sacrifice this same son. Again, he trusted God to, somehow, come through on His promise that this son would be the father of a great nation. So without question, he began to prepare the requested sacrifice! God's reward for his passing this test of faith was to provide him at the last minute with a ram for the *actual* sacrifice. Abraham, who became known to all Judeo-Christian believers as the Father of Faith, and his son Isaac, thus began the nation of Israel, and the Jewish bloodline through which Jesus was eventually born! (The story begins in Genesis 12.)

There were only three criteria that God had set for the candidate for this job: **steadfast faith in the promise**, which would be unaffected by a set of "impossible" circumstances; **undaunted patience**, which would come from trusting God's timing, even when the answer is delayed; and **unquestioning obedience** to God's instructions – even when they did not seem to make any sense. God wasn't looking for an extraordinary person, but for a common person with extraordinary faith, assured patience, and unhesitating obedience. That is still His criteria for His great servants today!

(The test of willingness to offer a son as a sacrifice was the foreshadowing of the sacrifice which God would later make for us. *He* never planned to actually make Abraham **pay** that price, but He knew that this would be the hardest instruction to ask any loving father to obey…to take the life of his own beloved son. Abraham trusted that God had a plan in mind, and that Isaac would live, because there was a long-standing promise attached to his life. His obedience validated his being chosen as the *right* man for this assignment!)

Surely, people thought Abraham was crazy to believe a promise of fathering a child at his age. Surely, they thought Noah was insane to begin building an enormous boat, when it had never rained. And just as assuredly, God included these and other similar accounts in the Bible for one reason—to impress upon us that He is a God of His word! His promises have **substance** to them…the "substance of things hoped for," which creates the substance of our faith!

Jesus' teachings on faith

If we examine what Jesus' life taught us about faith, we see that His healing power wasn't limited to only those who had faith for it. He sometimes, out of mercy, healed those who didn't even know who He was (John 5:2). But, the Bible focuses mainly on teaching us about those who did reach out **in faith**, in order to inspire us to do the same. Jesus said repeatedly to those who received healing, "Your faith has made you whole" (Luke 8:48;7:50; Mark 10:52;5:34; Matthew 9:22).

He revealed this to several people who were blind, to some who needed to be forgiven of sins, and to a woman who had been bleeding for 12 years, who merely touched the hem of His robe. In each of these cases, the faith itself was the **catalyst** which triggered the manifestation of the desired result. Jesus did *not* say to them, "I will perform this miracle for you because of your faith." Instead, He made the radical statement that **their faith itself** had **drawn** the miracle *to* them, *through* Him!

In the case of the woman with the issue of blood, Jesus never even saw her, He simply felt a drain of his healing virtue, and asked "Who touched me?" By the time He had asked the question, she was already healed. He told her that it was her faith that had healed her. She certainly wasn't the only one touching Him! He was being mobbed by people who were all wanting something from Him; she simply was the only one who was *absolutely certain* that He was so holy, that if she could just touch any part of Him, she would be healed. It wasn't the touch, but the believing, that made the difference.

In Jesus' time, the masses of people who witnessed His miracles and heard His teachings told others about it, who told others, and – eventually – many who heard about Him were able to believe that they, too, could be healed by the power of God which flowed through this Man. Some hoped it was true, and others KNEW it was true. Their spirits bore witness to the truth of it. Those who had **great**

faith received miracles which were not inhibited by either time or space (see Luke 7:1-10; Mark 5:21-43; Matthew 15:21-28; John 21:1-12, Luke 7:11-16). Since Jesus is as alive today, as He was on the day of His ascension, He is still able to perform miracles without regard to time or space! In the natural world "seeing is believing." In the things of the Spirit, "believing is seeing"!

What Jesus taught about the lack of faith

The most compelling message about absence of faith was when Jesus was walking on water in the storm, and Peter asked Him, "Lord, if it's You, tell me to come to You on the water" (Matthew 14:28 NIV). Most of us know the story...Jesus said "Come," Peter got out of the boat and started walking on the water toward Him, but then became afraid of the wind and started sinking. Jesus caught him and said, "You of little faith, why did you doubt?"

By including this experience in the Bible, God is showing us that the one in whom we have faith is right there with us, and isn't going to let us drown. We simply have to keep our eyes on Him, rather than on the storm that we are going through! It also illustrates that there is *only so much* that God is able to do for us when we are not exercising our faith. He has designed this spiritual universe to be interactive and inter-dependent. It really does take "two to tango" if you want to see the miraculous in your life! Our part is to BELIEVE! ("Be not afraid. Only believe." Mark 5:36)

Even Jesus, Himself, was hindered by the lack of faith *of other people*! In His hometown (where people still just thought of Him as "Joseph and Mary's boy"), the Scriptures say that He could do "few miracles" because of their unbelief. "He was amazed at their lack of faith" (Mark 6:5 NIV). This is especially true today, where so much of the world believes that Jesus was merely a "great prophet," but not the Messiah. As one Bible teacher accurately puts it, "You can believe and receive, or doubt and do without!"

[Have you ever wondered why the majority of Jews did not accept Jesus as the Messiah? ("He came unto His own, but His own received Him not" John 1:11) In Jesus' days, anyone who was hearing the Old Testament **with an open heart** would have realized that He was the fulfillment of prophecy, and that the Bible contained two distinctly different portrayals of the Messiah (coming once in sorrow and rejection, and then again in triumph). But the Word tells us that the hearts of most of the Jewish people were closed deliberately by God so that the Gentiles could receive the Messiah (see Romans 11:25). The next verses (26-36) assure us that "all of Israel will be saved," after all of the Gentiles have come in. Jews do not believe this, of course, but if God has ordained it, He will change their hearts, and it WILL come to pass!]

How to achieve greater faith

How is our faith increased? The most important clue that the Bible gives us is that "Faith comes by hearing, and hearing by the word of God" (Romans 10:17). There are any number of ways to hear about something, but this verse is telling us that there is only one **meaningful** way to "hear," and that is through the Word of God! And it tells us that the Word has been designated by our Creator to be the official transmitter by which faith is carried. If that is how faith "comes" (by hearing), then it follows that faith would **increase** by *practicing* the Word, and seeing it made manifest in our lives. The manifestations happen first in small ways, then in undeniably miraculous ways!

In this present day, Jesus isn't teaching and healing the masses in our streets. Reports on God's promises and miracle-working power may not be splashed in every day's headlines or on the nightly news. However, we are reminded of them every time we read the Bible or hear a meaningful sermon or personal testimony or listen to praise and worship music. "Hearing the Word of God" begins by exposing ourselves to it, but is accomplished in our hearts, more than in our ears. It is only through the work of the Holy Spirit that we can listen with our hearts!

It is difficult to trust someone that you don't know very well. But as you begin to draw near to God, through His Word, He will draw nearer to you (James 4:8). What kinds of things do we learn about God through the Bible? We learn such things as what grieves Him and what brings Him great joy; what a loving Father He is, and how He demonstrates it; and which character traits He values and those which He abhors. We learn every law that He expects us to obey and the consequences if we don't—as well as the blessings if we do! We learn how we can store up treasures in heaven, and what His plans are for this world. We see how many of His prophecies have already been fulfilled, and which are imminent. We learn to step out in faith on His promises, because the Word says: "God is not a man, that He should lie...hath He said, and shall He not do it?" (Hebrews 6:18).

We learn to distinguish His voice from the suggestions of the enemy and the desires of our flesh. Once we know His nature, whenever we have a thought or desire, we can test it by first asking ourselves, "Would God say that to me?" Jesus illustrated this in a parable referring to Himself, "and the sheep follow Him because they know His voice. And a stranger they will not follow...for they know not the voice of strangers" (John 10:4).

We also realize through studying the Word that God considers Himself to be in a covenant agreement with believers. The word testament *means* "covenant with God." In today's terminology, it would be called a contract. Webster's dictionary defines the word covenant as: "a formal, solemn and binding agreement." God made a covenant with the children of Israel when they came out of Egypt. "I will be your God, and you will be My people" (Leviticus 26:12). He kept His part of it, but they broke theirs...repeatedly. Jesus said at the Last Supper, "This is My blood of the new testament" (Matthew 26:28), a **NEW** agreement between man and God!

An agreement of any kind implies that each of the parties has an obligation to the other for some kind of performance. God has promised to fulfill **every** word He has spoken. Studying the Word will reveal to you what *your* part of the agreement is. Your faith will grow and flourish as you realize that He has singled **YOU** out of all mankind, to draw you into the safety and provision of His Covenant.

There is a beautiful verse in the Old Testament which promises, "And the LORD thy God will circumcise (cut away the hardened parts of) thine heart, and the heart of thy seed (your descendants), to love the LORD thy God with all thine heart, and with all thy soul, that thou mayest live" (Deuteronomy 30:6). If you find that your heart isn't as open toward God and His promises as you would like for it to be, then just ask Him to fulfill this Bible promise in your life, through the works of the Holy Spirit!

Another great way to build faith is to develop the habit of **remembering all of the wonderful things that God has done in your life**—or in the life of anyone close to you. Rehearse them in your mind, with a grateful heart! The Apostle Paul wrote to the Philippians: "Finally, brethren, whatsoever things are true, whatsoever things are honest, whatsoever things are just, whatsoever things are pure, whatsoever things are lovely, whatsoever things are of good report; and if there be any virtue, if there be any praise, think on these things" (4:8). This could even mean forcing yourself, when you are feeling too stressed to think of a blessing, to look out the window and say, "Look at that beautiful tree that God made!", then you can move into more personal gratitude.

Faith: the ultimate stress buster!

One of the most rewarding by-products of increased faith is the reduction of stress in our lives! Medical science now has reams of documented evidence that **emotional stress dramatically impairs immune function.** (They could have just asked the devil! He has learned from thousands of years of practice, that the easiest way to trigger chronic and terminal disease in humans, is simply to keep their minds filled with thoughts of fear and anger and rejection, and then he can just stand back and watch their immune systems self-destruct!) The medical community, of course, has no explanation for this weakness in our bodies…they just know that it happens.

I had a talk with God about that once. I asked Him, "How can it be…that, these bodies which You created to withstand all manner of physical assault [it can repair its own wounds, flush out toxins, maintain a constant temperature (until it needs to burn out a virus!), regenerate certain organs, kick in extra adrenaline for the "fight or flight response"]…HOW CAN IT BE that these self-monitoring machines cannot tolerate emotional stress? Did you forget something when You were at the drawing board, LORD?"

The Lord placed the following answer in my spirit: NO, He hadn't dropped the ball in the design process, but had deliberately **NOT** programmed us to be able to endure long-term emotional stress for several reasons:

1. His original intention was that man would live a harmonious, blessed life, free from the knowledge of evil. (God did not invent stress, we did!)

2. We are equipped to deal with certain physical challenges to our bodies, but **not** the challenges to our hearts. Why? Because we are supposed to take those to HIM, in prayers of faith, and **trust** Him to handle them! He has given us dozens of verses, which instruct us to do just that.

   "Cast your cares on the LORD and he will sustain you" (Psalms 55:22)

   "As for God, His way is perfect: the Word of the Lord

74

is tried: He is a buckler to all those who trust in Him" (Psalm 18:30)

"Trust in the Lord with all your heart, and lean not on your own understanding. In all your ways acknowledge Him and He shall direct your paths" (Proverbs 3:5,6)

"For your Heavenly Father knows that you need all these things. But seek first the Kingdom of God and His righteousness, and all these things shall be added unto you" (Matthew 6:28-33)

Give the things that trouble you to the Lord, and thank Him daily (or hourly, if you need to) for taking care of them, or for guiding you through them! Then, BELIEVE that He will do it.

3. He commanded for us a day of Sabbath rest (see Exodus 20:8), to be spent entirely with Him, so that our bodies and spirits could recharge once a week. Included here, also, would be the wisdom that we are expected to exercise in the care and feeding of our bodies. ("What! Know ye not that your bodies are the temple of the Holy Spirit?" (1 Corinthians 6:19).)

It would probably take a major restructuring of American society to set aside an entire day of restful time with God. But the Orthodox Jews still do a pretty good job of it, and they live in the same world that we do. (They strictly observe their Sabbath from sundown Friday, until sundown Saturday.)

God tells us that our "traditions" make His word of no effect (Matthew 15:6). This means that our habitual words, habitual thoughts, and habitual actions, which are not in agreement with His Word, actually nullify His promises. (When we break our part of the contract, the beneficial conditions of the contract are no longer in effect.) Then, we wonder why our prayers aren't answered! The next time you are standing in faith on a promise of God, examine the thoughts and words which you have allowed to dominate your mind during the *other* 23 hours of the day!

Guard your heart

To minimize stress in your life, learn to guard your heart (and your eyes and ears) from things that are designed by the enemy to chip away at your faith, and to draw you into fear, lust, and inner turmoil. "Keep thy heart with all diligence, for out of it are the issues of life" (Proverbs 4:23).

Guarding your heart would include resisting the "downloading" of any material which is contradictory to God's Word, into your soul. (This could be in the form of books, movies, soap operas, television shows, chat rooms, etc...you know which ones they are!) Your faith *is* affected by continuing to embrace *worldly* escapism as a source of comfort or distraction. Faith isn't something that is independent and separate from the rest of you. The Word says that: "A double-minded man is unstable in all his ways" (James 1:8). The truth is that there are carnal Christians and spiritual Christians. We are not expected by God to be perfect (we all sin and fall short of the glory of God everyday (Romans 3:23)), but we *are* expected to decide which world we are going to call "home," and (if it is His kingdom) to stay there!

God has called us to: "Come out from among them, and be ye separate" (2 Corinthians 6:17). He will help us to do it. It is *not* too late for anyone! Jesus said to Simon Peter in Luke 22:31: "Simon, Simon, behold, Satan has desired to have you, that he may sift you like wheat. But I have prayed for thee, <u>that thy faith fail not</u>; and when thou art converted, strengthen thy brethren."

Peter went on to betray Jesus by denying Him three times, yet Jesus drew Peter back to Himself, and made him one of the leaders of the early Christian Church.

This verse resonates with me at a personal level, because the devil tried to sift me like wheat for most of my life – and I betrayed God by my conduct and my beliefs, but here I am: born again, and attempting to strengthen my brethren!

If you gave up on God – only once or a million times – God hasn't given up on you! There is faith, deep inside of you. Just STIR IT UP!

"God hath dealt to every man the measure of faith" (Romans 12:3)

"Wherefore I put thee in remembrance that thou stir up the gift of God, which is in thee by the putting on of my hands. For God hath not given us the spirit of fear, but of power and of love and of a sound mind" (2 Timothy 1:6,7)

The Bible says that in the end times, men's hearts will be failing them for fear, and for dreading of what will happen next (see Luke 21:26). If the play-by-play coverage of world events by the news media tends to make you nervous or depressed, then consider cutting back on your exposure to it. We want to be informed about what is going on (for one thing, we need to know what to pray about), but a constant diet of words and images which focus on the problems and tragedies of the world can be used by the devil to traumatize us (especially if we are not listening with our "spiritual ears"). It can become difficult to hear God's still, small voice speaking into our spirits (see 1 Kings 19:11-13).

If we have read the end of The Book, then we know where we are headed. We must set our faces "like flint" (Isaiah 50:7) to trust God to know what He is doing, and to show us what our roles are in it, and how to pray. What is the worst thing that can happen to us—that we step out of these bodies and into His arms?

[If you have no knowledge of Bible prophecy, you may want to read: *Are We Living in The Last Days?* by Tim LaHaye and Jerry Jenkins.]

Should you decide to cut back on any media pass-time, then perhaps you could commit that half-hour, or hour, in the morning and evening to devotional time…quality reserved time, rather than "catch as catch can." When we make choices like this, God rewards us with increased blessings and increased faith! The psalmist David wrote: "My voice Thou shalt hear in the morning, O LORD" (Psalms 5:3, also 63:1;143:8;1 Samuel 1:19). Beginning your day with God's Word will set the course for a day of peace and assurance, and will help you to be focused on staying in His will for that day, rather than focused on the problems of the world.

Have faith in the will of God

A friend recently sent me an anonymous prayer, which contains a pleasant reminder in every line. I will share it with you, in belief that God will use it to encourage you in your walk of faith, especially if you are going through a "trial" or if your faith is being tested!

The Will of God

The will of God will never take me,
Where the grace of God cannot keep me,
Where the arms of God cannot support me,
Where the riches of God cannot supply my needs,
Where the power of God cannot endow me.

The will of God will never take me,
Where the Spirit of God cannot work through me
Where the wisdom of God cannot teach me,
Where the army of God cannot protect me,
Where the hands of God cannot mold me.

The will of God will never take me,
Where the love of God cannot enfold me,
Where the mercies of God cannot sustain me,
Where the peace of God cannot calm my fears,
Where the authority of God cannot overrule for me.

The will of God will never take me,
Where the comfort of God cannot dry my tears,

Where the Word of God cannot feed me,
Where the miracles of God cannot be done for me,
Where the omnipresence of God cannot find me.

Everything happens for a purpose.
We may not see the wisdom of it now,
But trust and believe in the Lord
That everything is for the best.

If you can believe that He DOES have a perfect will for your life, then you will soon be able to surrender to that will in faith. Continue to trust Him, and to exercise the degree of faith which you DO have. Soon your faith will begin to deepen and expand. It will conquer the spirits of fear and doubt. One day, you will find yourself believing for things which you would have never thought possible! It is through acts of faith that God will walk you out of your adverse circumstances.

According to Mark 11:22, Jesus said, "Have faith in God," but the literal translation in Greek is, "Have the faith OF God." Ultimately it IS possible to reach the point of having the faith OF God, not just faith IN God.

How confident do you suppose GOD is, that you can trust His will for you?

Chapter Six
Is God still answering prayer?

God impressed upon me one day that anyone who prays, DOES believe in miracles...whether they admit it or not! How could anything less than a miracle account for the fact that the God of the universe is actually willing and able to zero in on the minutiae of our lives, hearing our spoken and unspoken prayers? We are already describing a miracle of mass proportions, and we haven't yet mentioned the fact that not only are our prayers HEARD, but they are ANSWERED! The answer might not always be "yes," and it might not always be immediate, but God always answers His mail!

You are not just an anonymous being, sending up a prayer that may or may not hit its target. As a Christian, you have your own private "Dream Team" (Father, Son and Holy Spirit) desiring to be in constant relationship with you! We each have the privilege of being loved (as though we were an only child) by a God who is so vast that there is more than enough of Him to go around. God has taught me this truth, both through a word of revelation knowledge and through my personal experience with Him. To embrace the reality of it is both life transforming and prayer transforming!

The answer to the title question is, "YES, God is still answering prayer. This verse in 2 Chronicles 16:9 is as true today as it was the day it was written: "For the eyes of the LORD run to and fro throughout the whole earth, to show Himself strong in the behalf of them whose heart is perfect toward Him." There you have it…He **wants** to do things for you, and to make a difference in your life! We can't say this too many times: He is not looking for perfect people (thank God!), but He is looking for those who believe who He is, what He says, and who want to be in relationship with Him.

Some dear people don't feel comfortable asking God for anything. They assume that if God wanted you to have something, that you would already have it! It is true that God has blessed us all in innumerable ways, and that He knows our thoughts and the desires of our hearts. But none of those things really require us to be in **relationship** with Him, and that is what He desires most! He enjoys hearing that we know His promises, and has invited us to come "boldly before His throne" (Hebrews 4:16). He also encourages us: "with thanksgiving, let your requests be made known unto God" (Philippians 4:6,7), and says that we have not because we ask not (James 4:2).

When it seems that prayers aren't being answered

Even during those times when your prayers seem to be falling back to earth, unanswered, be assured that they are being heard loud and clearly. At these times, God is probably doing one of two things: Either He is waiting for YOU to do something that you haven't done (which could be to pray within the confines of His Word), or

He is waiting for His perfect timing in bringing together all of the pieces, and in connecting all the dots, and in moving all the other related lives and circumstances into position regarding your situation. He is working behind the scenes, even when you don't see anything happening! God also waits until we are in the perfect place in our spiritual growth to be able to receive and maintain a specific blessing, without being in danger of backsliding once we have it. We have no recourse, but to learn to wait on God, and keep ourselves in a position to receive! "But they that wait upon the Lord shall renew their strength, they shall mount up with wings as eagles, they shall run and not be weary, and they shall walk and not faint" (Isaiah 40:31).

Praying "within the confines of His Word" would mean that you are familiar enough with the Bible to know those things which are NOT okay to ask for, and which things are always in His will. It would mean that you have examined yourself to make certain that you are not standing on the hose through which your blessing would flow, by entertaining a sin such as unforgiveness. And it would mean that you have arrived at that place in your heart where you are willing to say, "Not my will, but Thine be done" (Matthew 6:9). You will know that you have arrived at a new level, spiritually, when you stop asking God to bless and approve YOUR plans, but ask Him to guide you into HIS plan for your life!

Even then, He may not reveal an entire plan to you, but just encourage you to take the next step or move toward the next door. If that one opens, move toward the next door! If it doesn't open, then pray for wisdom as to whether or not this plan is of God, or to be given peace in your heart as you continue to pray and wait on the Lord.

Remember – God doesn't work by our time clock, but by the eternal "big picture." He doesn't reveal that picture, or our entire future, to us because it is not the destination that is important to Him—it is our journey with Him.

Is it okay to ask Him more than once?

Assuming that we are praying within His will (1 John 5:14-15), then there is nothing in the Bible that suggests that repeating a righteous prayer is indicative of lack of faith. On the contrary, the Bible seems to suggest that we should persevere with prayer and not give up until we have the answer! Why else would we be commanded to "Pray without ceasing" (1 Thessalonians 5:17), and that "Men ought always to pray and not to faint" (Luke 18:1-8)?

Jesus gave us two parables to illustrate this principle. One is His story about a neighbor who came calling at midnight. He was finally given three loaves of bread (which he wanted for his visitor) simply because he *persisted* in asking (Luke 11:5-8). The other parable is about a non-believing judge who finally gave up (and gave in) in dealing with a distraught woman who persevered about wanting to receive justice from her adversary. The parable continues, "and will God not bring about justice for His chosen ones, who cry out to him day and night?" (Luke 18:1-8).

The above parables are God's way of telling us that, whether we are praying in behalf of someone else (as in seeking "bread" for the visitor...*three* loaves...get it?) or seeking our own deliverance and restitution from attacks of the devil ("justice from the adversary"), if we (His chosen ones) persist in prayer, God will bring it to pass! (Don't wonder if that includes you. You are reading this book *because* you have been chosen! "You have not chosen Me, I have chosen you" John 15:16.)

Jesus delighted in speaking in parables for the same reason that God delights in using "the (seemingly) foolish things" of this world to "confound the wise" (1 Corinthians 1:27)! Matters of the Spirit can only be understood by those who are true seekers of the Kingdom of God. This realm operates on a different set of laws, and the "lingo" is only comprehended after one becomes a citizen of the Kingdom! Jesus was willing to explain His parables only to believers, and not to the rest of the world—He left the others just shaking their heads in bewilderment.

God tells us, " for as the heavens are higher than the earth, so are My ways higher than your ways, and My thoughts than your thoughts" (Isaiah 55:9). To which I have often said, "No kidding, Lord! And they are often the *reverse* of our thoughts!" For example, in the Kingdom, you go lower (become more humble) in order to go higher. You give away what you have, in order to have more! Who would guess that a busy God would suggest that we are to keep returning to Him with the same prayers? Yet, He does, for His own profound reason. (He doesn't want just "vain repetitions" (Matthew 6:7), but promises that "the fervent prayers of a righteous man avail much" (1 John 5:14).)

Some might ask: "If Christians are saved, justified and sanctified, why would we have to keep begging God for something?" This is where it would come in handy to have a more comprehensive knowledge of Scripture, and not just of isolated verses. All of God's Word works together. As Christians, we are not begging God in our prayers, but praying in faith. Never forget that heaven and earth are interactive! God didn't *have* to make it that way, but He obviously *chose* to involve us in the process by the exercising of our faith.

If you want an earthly comparison, think of a company whose employees are also major stockholders. These employees have a greater than average interest in the daily operations of the company. They also have a greater sense of responsibility, a greater sense of peace, feel closer to the management, and receive greater benefits than employees who just work at a "job" and who have no investment in the end result. (The vested employees still have to remember, however, *who* is in charge!) The same things are true of believers who exercise their "option" to play a role in the "business" of the heavenlies. God is still in charge, but when we take Him up on His invitation of using our prayers to effect change, then we have greater responsibility in our own lives, greater peace, feel closer to God, and see greater blessings!

We can learn to pray – NOT in desperation, or frustration, or fear – but in quiet confidence that God is *using* our prayers of faith to accomplish *His* purposes!

How God uses our prayers of faith

I didn't fully comprehend this concept, until I read the book *Reese Howells, Intercessor*, a biography by Norman Grubb. Mr. Howells was mightily used by God in England in the early 1900s. (An intercessor is someone who prays in behalf of others.) The entire account of his life is inspirational to anyone with a heart or an anointing for intercession. After I had finished reading it, the Lord specifically sent me back to re-read a small portion which was found in the last few pages. This portion wasn't necessarily the most impressive act of intercession in the book, but it was the one that contained the lesson which the Holy Spirit wanted to drive deep into my spirit.

He had me read those lines again and again, until I had memorized the operative sentence. It was from a journal entry which Mr. Howells had written while he was interceding for the British troops during the Battle of Britain. The British army was the decided underdog and seemed to be headed for certain defeat, as Mr. Howells pressed in, **believing** that his prayers *would* be used by God to make a difference.

One monumental day, the tide was turned in the spiritual realm. Britain was assured of victory, even though it wasn't manifested until several days later. This was Mr. Howells' journal entry for that day: **"The Holy Ghost has found faith equal to what *He* wants to do."**

The Holy Spirit emblazoned those words on my heart! God actually has things which He wants to accomplish, which are being so vigorously opposed by the enemy, that the situation won't change unless someone with GREAT faith—who **believes** the notion that God will take that faith and physically USE it—keeps praying in undeterred faith! Not because God **can't** change it, but because it involves something in the heavenlies which He has preordained to respond to our participation, and to our choices of either faith or doubt.

During the Battle of Britain, Winston Churchill wrote in his *War Memoirs* that the German bombers and fighters began turning for home just at the moment when victory was in their grasp. There seemed to be no reason. The British army had no more reserves. God had altered the course of history! Reese Howells wrote in his journal, "You can't trust in anything except believing prayer." "What if millions of prayers went up and no one had believed?"

"Praying-through" in intercession

It is obvious that God doesn't merely respond to **need,** or there would be no need in the world. He *does* respond to faith, and then weaves it into the fabric of His other considerations, such as timing, and His ultimate plan. Satan the accuser never takes a vacation from condemning us before God for our prior sins – which is why we need a Savior. He never stops trying to maneuver the world toward disaster, by encouraging spiritually weak people to do diabolical acts. So, we must never take a vacation from offering prayers to be used to off-set him, and to pull things back to being spiritually on-course with God's perfect will! God doesn't actually NEED our help, but if we are so complacent as to be willing to just let everything "go to hell in a hand-basket," then the devil has a legal right to grab that basket and run with it.

I don't presume to understand ALL of the spiritual implications and mechanics of it, I just know that when **God** gives me a clear instruction to pray and believe for something and the faith to stand for it – then it is a done deal. You can take it to the bank. It is GOING to happen, no matter what it looks like or how long it takes! I am NOT going to relinguish the reason that He has entrusted me with this kind of faith – I know that I will "use it or loose it!"

Since my experience with the Reese Howells book, there have been times when God has lead me to "pray-through" some really difficult situations. These times are as close as I have come to praying "without ceasing". I pray aloud, pray silently, pray in the Spirit, worship, praise, stand on verses of Scripture, and give thanks *until* I hear the Holy Spirit say, "GRANTED!" This means praying while driving, while bathing, while shopping, while cooking, and as I fall asleep at night. I have done it for as little as 10 minutes, and for as long as three weeks, before hearing "DONE!" After hearing that, I am flooded with a huge wave of relief and I can no longer pray, except to offer praise and thanksgiving. I receive a peace that is rock solid, whether or not the result can be seen yet in the physical. At times, praying-through a situation has involved storming the gates of hell, confidently exclaiming, "NOOOOO, Satan, this WILL NOT happen! You can FORGET IT!" as I turn to God and remind Him of all His promises, and let Him know that I trust Him.

Of course, **not** all intercessory prayer has to be this intense and protracted. Many of my prayers for others are a one-time, but heart-felt and expectant, conversation with God, where I simply invite Him to give me the words to pray. I also pray that He is preparing the heart of the person being prayed for to be a willing recipient and that His perfect will, *will* be revealed and followed.

What are the basic essentials of personal prayer?

This book is designed to be a primer, containing some basic principles of Christianity, which may not have been adequately presented to you before now. The topic of every chapter and every subtext which we have discussed could be (and undoubtedly *has* been) expanded into a lengthy book of its own. But, in this section, the same could be said for every **paragraph**, for there is much to be taught about meaningful prayer!

We don't want to get into legalism, however, and dictate how you must pray. All communication with God is good! Rest assured, that He loves hearing from you, no matter the time, place, circumstance, form, or style. All that really matters is that you seek Him with your whole heart, fully believing that He hears and will answer you! If you and God have a great prayer relationship, then keep it that way, until He leads you into desiring to do something differently.

I will share with you a brief synopsis of a few Bible-based points which I have come to understand about prayer. Perhaps the Holy Spirit will quicken you to increase your prayer power and your intimacy with Him by including some of the following:

Praying in the name of Jesus

You know, of course, that as Christians, we always petition the Father in the name of Jesus. We must be careful to never fall into the practice of using His name merely as a required recitation (as in the manner of flashing your membership card at Sam's Club)! It is true that using the name of Jesus DOES get you "in" to a privileged place, but never forget what is behind the power of His name (the work of the Cross) and behind the purpose of praying in His name: "and whatsoever ye ask in My name, that will I do, that the Father may be glorified in the Son" (John 14:13).

Waiting on God

Whenever possible, before beginning to pray, wait to feel a oneness with God. (The more often you do this, the more quickly it comes!) Waiting for the presence of the Holy Spirit is not simply waiting for a tingling numbness (or however your physical barometer measures His presence). You are not asking "Come, Holy Spirit", merely in order to feel anointed or to have a greater chance that your prayer will be heard and answered (although both of these will occur), but to invite Him to lead and guide you in your prayer. It is possible to use these moments of waiting on God to clear your heart and mind of all motives save being one with the Father, just as He was one with Jesus during His time on earth (John 17:6-26). Being in one mind with the Father is asking **Him** to GIVE you the words to pray.

Using the Lord's Prayer as a guide

When Jesus taught His disciples "how to pray" (Matthew 6:9-13), there were many deep, metaphoric symbols within the text, but it also gave us a basic outline of elements which can be considered when we approach the Father in prayer:

"Our Father in heaven...hallowed be thy name." We begin by remembering His position and revering His holiness.

"Thy kingdom come" We have just mentioned that we invite

91

His presence. Also, according to Matthew 25:34, we believers are heirs to the Kingdom of God. We are citizens of the Kingdom by virtue of having been born again of the Spirit of God. By speaking these words, we are affirming that we want that Kingdom to increase in our lives and on this earth. Remember what kingdom you belong to as you are praying!

"Thy will be done on earth as it is in heaven." We refrain from praying for things that would be outside of His will and His Word. This doesn't mean that you can't ask for the dreams and desires of your heart—He probably put them there! But it would exclude selfish ambition and unwillingness to follow the path and the purpose for which He created you. This line of Scripture also lets us know that we do NOT have to wait until we get to heaven to know the things of God. His perfect will *can* be accomplished here, "**as it is in heaven**"!

"Give us this day our daily bread." We are invited to ask God to bless us with all those things which He wants us to have. This would include the healing of our bodies. Jesus said (in Matthew 15:25) that healing is the children's (believers') "bread." Jesus also referred to Himself as the "Bread of Life." So, remember when you come to God in prayer, that it is not just *through* the Son, but also *because of* the Son, that God is so willing to entertain our petitions!

"Forgive our debts, as we forgive our debtors." This is the prayer with a "catch" to it, which many people pray (for all of their lives) without realizing. It is tied directly into the verses which are two lines below it. Failure to observe this warning from Jesus **may** result in your prayers falling on deaf ears! "For if ye forgive men their trespasses, your heavenly Father will also forgive you; But if ye forgive not men their trespasses, neither will your Father forgive your trespasses" (Matthew 6:14,15). This is such an important issue with God that we devoted all of Chapter Four to it in this book, and I will remind you of its punch-line: "Forgiveness? Just do it!"

The next two petitions in the Lord's Prayer have to do with keeping us protected from sin and evil. Remember before you pray, to make sure that your spiritual armor is in place (see Chapter Three)!

"Lead us not into temptation." Temptation does not come from God, but from Satan.

> "Let no one say when he is tempted, 'I am being tempted by God; for God cannot be tempted by evil, nor does He Himself tempt anyone. But each one is tempted when he is drawn away by his own desires and enticed. Then, when desire has conceived, it gives birth to sin; and sin, when it is full-grown, brings forth death." (1 John 2:15-17)

The desire comes from your flesh; the enticing is done by the devil. Jesus was tempted by the devil for 40 days in the wilderness (Mark 1:13). He told His disciples, "Pray that you may not enter into temptation" (Luke 22:40). We are all tempted, but not beyond what we are able to withstand (1 Corinthians 10:12). Remember, since Jesus is human, He knows our weaknesses, and He will help to "deliver the godly out of temptations" (Hebrews 4:15; 2 Peter 2:9). God will allow us to be TESTED, but it is the devil who tempts us. So, as you are praying, be aware of where the problem that you are praying about is really coming from!

"But deliver us from evil." Today, there is rapidly-increasing evil in the world all around us. Also, we just looked at the fact that there is evil *inside* of us. But, remember, Jesus didn't ask for the evil to not exist...the devil's lease isn't up yet!...He just told us to pray that we be **delivered out** of it. So, when we pray, rather than asking for our problems to disappear, we should ask for our Deliverer to guide us **through** them. We pray for Him to be in our situation with us...to be with us in every choice and in every move we make. We ask Him to help us to blaze a trail out of the predicament, without stepping on land mines or into quicksand (which could result from our trying to work our way out of it by our own devices.)

"For Thine is the Kingdom, the power and the glory forever." The Kingdom belongs to Him, the power belongs to Him, and the glory belongs to Him. That just about covers it, doesn't it? It all belongs to Him. Although we can enjoy Father-child intimacy with God, we should always remember that everything we have comes from Him. A truly complete prayer will express thankfulness for all that He has done for us and praise for His goodness!

Prayers of agreement

Your private prayer time alone with God is precious and fruitful, but when you are not seeing results (or are in urgent need of seeing God show up in a situation), remember the promise of power which is to be found in prayers of agreement. "When two or three are gathered in My name, there I am in the midst of them" (Matthew 18:20). Ask God to help you cultivate relationships with other strong believers so that you can pray for each others' needs and the needs of your church, of our country and the world. If you have no one to pray with you, then consider calling one of the numerous prayer lines that are available through Christian television, both locally and nationally. (Some are toll-free and they have anointed prayer warriors who will pray for you, with you standing in agreement.)

In Deuteronomy 32:30 we are told that one put a thousand to flight, and two put ten thousand to flight. That's pretty good math, in anyone's book! The addition of only one person resulted in tenfold increase in power!

Remember:
- Even Jesus asked His disciples to pray with Him in the garden of Gethsemane (Matthew 26:36-41).
- When Peter was in prison, the Church was praying for him in one accord, and an angel showed up and led him to freedom (Acts 12:7).
- Pentecost happened when 120 people were in one place and in one accord (Acts 2:1).
- In the book of Genesis (11:6 NIV), the people were of one mind and one language – and they liked it that way! So, they decided to stay put in Babylon and build a tower to heaven. But God realized that He had to break them up, and scatter them, and give them different languages, because their unity was causing them to focus on themselves, and to ignore His will. He said that, "If as one people speaking the same language, they

have begun to do this, then nothing that they plan to do will be impossible for them."

They had accidentally stumbled onto one of those universal truths which God had set into motion: There is power in unity – in being of one mind! Unfortunately, it works both for those in unity for good and for those in unity for the opposite.

The forces of evil seem to have no problem in being of one accord. If the Body of Christ would come into similar agreement, there would be nothing that we couldn't accomplish for God!

Prayer and Fasting

Fasting is a practice which has probably become more popular in the secular world, than it has in the Christian world! Health-seekers have caught on to its benefits in regard to cleaning out the body, and allowing the energy which would have gone into the digesting of food to be used elsewhere. Other religions have long embraced the fact that it helps to clear the mind and enables one to focus on things more "spiritual" than physical.

Many Christians seem to have the notion that fasting is an Old Testament or archaic practice, which would not have any significance today, but it is taught in both the Old and New Testaments. Jesus, Himself fasted, and He instructed us that "when (*not "IF"*) ye fast, be not as the hypocrites, of a sad countenance..." In other words, do this, but don't act like you are holier-than-thou and suffering. No one needs to know that you are fasting, but God!

Fasting is abstaining from some or all food (or some other pleasure), for a spiritual purpose. It is a gift that we offer to God which indicates our willingness to deny our physical needs, in order to pursue Him and our spiritual needs. The Bible speaks of fasts of 3, 14, 20, or 40 days, but God may lead you to fast one meal a day, or one day a week. If you are fasting solid foods, you may drink juices, or one of the many nutritional drinks which are now available in health food stores.

Fasting is not merely abstinence, but the setting aside of that time and energy in order to give yourself to prayer, and to meditation on God's will. A prolonged fast should never be undertaken, however, simply out of a sense of duty or without a clear leading by the Lord to do so. God commanded fasting on the Jewish Day of Atonement ("*deny yourself*"), but in Isaiah 58 He clarifies the meaning of it. He says that it is not merely for repentance and humbling oneself, but is undertaken in order to **take on** those things which we have *not* been doing—such as feeding and clothing and giving shelter to the poor, and helping your own family. In other words, in fasting, we should not be preoccupied with twisting God's arm to do something for *us*! Instead, we should be focused on cleansing ourselves of those physical and spiritual things which interfere with our hearing God and doing His work here on earth. "Create in me a new heart and renew a steadfast spirit within me" (Psalms 51:10). Of course, it is no coincidence that prayers are usually answered as the result of a proper fast. It is another one of those "excuses" God finds to give us a blessing!

Praise and Worship

Psalm 22:3 tells us that "God inhabits the praises of His people and fills us with His presence." In other words, when we praise, He shows up! This is why, in many churches (large and small) and in great crusades where believers are focused on expressing their love for the Lord, an atmosphere is created which the Holy Spirit cannot resist being a part of! Worshippers can be healed and restored and set free from bondage just by being present in the anointing which descends on the wings of fervent praise and worship!

It doesn't have to be quiet and solemn (Psalm 149 says to "praise Him in the dance, with timbrel and harp"), it can be joyous and loud; but whatever the tone or tempo, it is a time to forget our own needs, and be attentive to blessing Him. How do we bless God? Nothing blesses God more than to hear His people celebrating His only begotten Son. But we also bless Him with thanksgiving, and by acknowledging all that He has done. There is even something called "the sacrifice of praise" (Hebrews 13:15), which means that even when we don't feel like it, we praise Him ANYWAY! As a matter of fact, if you really want to get God's attention, make it a habit to praise Him when things **aren't** going well…to let Him know that *you* know that He's good *all* the time, and that He's trying to help you *all* the time, not just when you can see the positive manifestations of it.

There is every conceivable type of praise and worship music available on CD today, which (when combined with your heart) can draw the presence of the Holy Spirit into your home. If you want God to feel comfortable in your house, and to be present even before you begin to you pray, then you can invite Him by playing "His kind of music"!

David the Psalmist ("a man after God's own heart" Acts 13:22) gave us so much material to work with in the area of praising God! Perhaps we should take our cue from the fact that he was beloved and highly favored of God because of his heart for Him. David worshipped the Lord with unabashed adoration. He committed some pretty serious offenses, but God called him a "righteous man" because "love covers a multitude of sins" (Proverbs 10:2).

These few verses of David are a great place to begin the practice of offering praises to the Lord:

> "I will bless the LORD at all times, His praise shall continually be in my mouth." (Psalms 34:1)

> "Make a joyful noise unto the LORD, all ye lands. Serve the LORD with gladness, come before His presence with singing. Know ye that the LORD He is God: it is He that hath made us, not we ourselves; we are His people and the sheep of His pasture. Enter into His gates with thanksgiving and into His courts with praise: be thankful unto Him, and bless His name. For the LORD is good; His mercy is everlasting; and His truth endureth to all generations." (Psalm 100)

Final Thoughts on Prayer

The evidence of God's willingness to answer prayer has been the subject of several scientific studies in the past two decades. One study in 1988 concluded that patients who were prayed for (by people who believed in God and in healing) were released from the hospital sooner than those who were not prayed for.

The result of a 1999 study at St. Luke's Hospital in Kansas City were published with the conclusion that "Prayer may be an effective adjunct to standard medical care."

I wonder how God feels about having His attentiveness toward mankind being quantitatively measured by scientists. When we remember how determined He seems to be to confound those who *think* they are wise, we might assume that He is not interested in performing for the press or in having people turn to Him simply because it has been scientifically proven that He exists. That would eliminate the need for faith – God's gold standard!

Jesus said in John 20 "Blessed are those who have believed, but not seen." He would probably prefer that we each discover for ourselves that He *does* answer prayer!

Chapter Seven

What must I do to be saved and walking with God?

Having that desire is the first step, because God sees your heart. Your intentions are far more important than your words!

Salvation

There is no Biblical necessity of, or set wording for, a prayer of salvation. So, why do all preachers lead you through one? Because God calls us to be pro-active with our faith, and because we must speak our intention. A relationship with God is never something to be passive about – but where salvation is concerned, the benefit is worth making certain that God knows that you are serious about it! ("He is a rewarder of them that diligently seek Him" Hebrews 11:6)

The requirements established by Jesus for salvation are that you believe in Him and acknowledge that belief to others. "Whosoever shall confess Me before men, him shall the Son of man also confess before the angels of God" (Luke 12:8). In Romans 10:10, the Word states: "If thou shalt confess with thy mouth the Lord Jesus, and believe in your heart that God hath raised Him from the dead, thou shalt be saved."

Salvation is a gift which is received *by grace through faith.* In other words, if you really mean your prayer, you will receive salvation, without deserving or paying for it, simply because God says so! Grace is divine benevolence which is lovingly bestowed on those who don't merit it, but whom God can't resist blessing and saving. He wants with all His heart to bless you with the gift of eternal life and forgiveness of sins, and He went to great lengths to create a plan which would be simple to accept, yet still involve a conscious choice on your part.

He has always desired to save and bless and forgive mankind, but we haven't always made it exactly easy for Him to convey these gifts and still be able to maintain spiritual order. Two thousand years ago, He gave up on our ever getting it right (He knew we wouldn't) and made it available to us simply through His *grace!*

We are all familiar with the concept of a grace period. For example, if you don't pay your utility bill on time, they don't immediately turn off your electricity. Even though you haven't kept your part of the bargain, the power company will treat you as though you were "innocent" for ten more days. God's grace period of treating you as though you are innocent began when He sent His Son to the Cross. And this grace period has no termination date.

Your part of the bargain is to accept the terms of the agreement:
"Therefore if anyone is in Christ, he is a new creation; the old has gone, the new has come! All this is from God, who reconciled us to Himself in Christ, not counting men's sins against them…We implore you

on Christ's behalf: Be reconciled to God. God made Him who had no sin to be sin for us, so that in Him we might become the righteousness of God." (2 Corinthians 5:17-21)

God sent His only-begotten Son to carry out a plan, which would result in your debt (of disobedient thoughts, words and deeds) being marked "cancelled/paid in full"…just by accepting His gift into your heart. Understand: it is a debt that you could have *never* paid. Once you have accepted the truth of this "intellectually unlikely" scenario, the Holy Spirit will place a peaceful certainty about it in your heart. You will *know* that you will be spending eternity in the best of all possible worlds—the Kingdom of Heaven—rather than where you would have been if judged by your own merits. The unseen things and promises of God are *more real* than this page which you are holding and reading!

Perhaps at this moment, you *are* interested in knowing that you will go to heaven when you die, but aren't particularly concerned about the spiritual quality of the remainder of your life here on earth. You might prefer to merely say, "Okay, Jesus, I believe in You. Forgive my sins, come into my life, and let's get on with it!" If that is all the enthusiasm that you can muster, then, I assure you, He will honor it, work with you, and you might be as saved as I am…but it may be a long while before you see any appreciable change in the quality of your life!

You probably have a lot of living to do before going on to heaven! You will see some impressive changes and will be prepared to be effective for the Kingdom if you come before God with a sincere desire that the words you pray will grow inside of you and transform the remainder of your life through the abiding presence of the Holy Spirit! Your life may not become "charmed," but it will become more meaningful, more connected to God and your fellow man, more peaceful, and you will never again have reason to fear death. You will also know the unconditional love which has long evaded you…and that's just the *beginning* of the journey!

The prayer below is what the Lord gave me, and it seems to cover all the bases of what (according to the Bible) God would have us believe in our hearts. You might want to read it first, silently, and see if your spirit connects with it. If so, pray it aloud or ask God or a friend to give you a meaningful prayer of salvation. This longer prayer won't make you "more saved" than a shorter one will, but it might bring your heart and mind more into agreement with your spirit!

A prayer of salvation and rebirth

Father, thank You for loving me unconditionally and for opening my heart to wanting more of You. I come before You with a repentant heart. I have sinned against You in more ways than I can call to mind, but You know – and will forgive – them all! I repent for, and ask You to help me turn from, everything that has ever separated me from You.

Thank You, God, for sending a part of Yourself—God the Word—to be born into flesh on this earth as Your Only Begotten Son, and to suffer and die on a cross, so that I may receive forgiveness, peace, salvation and healing of body and soul.

Thank You for raising Jesus from death to life, in victory, on the third day and for drawing Him by ascension to live with You in heaven, where He sits at Your right hand in glory.

Jesus, I am asking You to come into my heart and into my life. Thank You for cleansing and purifying my heart. Thank You for dying so that I may live. Thank You for truly being my Savior!

Thank You for sending the Holy Spirit to reside inside of me, to reveal the truth of Jesus to me, and to endue me with His power.

Holy Spirit, I gratefully accept Your guidance and every spiritual gift You have to offer me!

Father, I willingly choose to die to the person I have been up to this moment of my life. I have tried it my way, and now I'm ready to try Your way! I offer the rest of my life to be guided by Your perfect will, that I may become the person You created me to be, in harmony and oneness with You.

Thank You for giving me the privilege and opportunity to be born again in this life, and, when it ends, to live eternally in Your presence, love and peace.

I believe this confession of the Gospel in my heart and will not be ashamed to declare it before men!

In Jesus' precious name, Amen.

Welcome to the Kingdom of God! If that (or a similar) prayer reflects what is in your heart, you are now saved and born again!

Please permit me now to share with you some things that may help you with your Christian walk.

Beginning your Christian walk

If you have just come to the Lord, then, please, take some time to bask in the warmth of God's grace toward you and in the glow of the amazing sacrificial gesture of love which Jesus has performed for you! He is no longer standing at the door knocking, He has taken up residence inside of you, through the Holy Spirit. So, as you seek to go deeper with Him, look for Him WITHIN you...deep within your spirit. May the reality of this miracle bring peace to your body and soul!

When you feel so led, ask the Holy Spirit to guide you into prayerful consideration of what *your* role will be in this covenant agreement. Not your *ultimate* purpose or assignment (yet!), but the degree to which you are willing to allow others to see Him in you, and through you!

In the discussion entitled "What Is Christianity?", we examined some of the probable reasons that not all Christians are operating in the peace, love and power that is available to them. It is certainly possible to believe in Jesus, without being in relationship with Him. But once you have invited Him to draw closer, God will begin to draw closer to you. You will find yourself desiring to make your walk with Him a two-way street.

You will no longer just be praying "Bless me, give me, help me, amen", but you will have acquired a heart of gratitude that recognizes the grace and mercy which He has shed on your life. It is at that point of experiencing true parent-child bonding with Papa God ("Abba Father," see Romans 8:15), that His, and Jesus', instructions to us no longer seem burdensome, and we actively seek His face —

not just His hand. We begin to see the Ten Commandments and Jesus' commandments as boundaries for our safekeeping, and as opportunities for us to demonstrate and reciprocate the unconditional love which has been showered on our lives! (In John 14:15, Jesus says, "If you love Me, keep My commandments.")

Just as well-nurtured and well-raised young children (eventually!) grow out of being "me"-oriented and self-obsessed, and into being mature, compassionate contributors to society, the same is true of well-taught and well-mentored "young" Christians—they become willing and eager to be transformed by God into effective contributors to the Kingdom, effective conduits of the love of Christ, and effective vessels to be used for God's purposes. For some new Christians, this happens at salvation; for others, it takes years; and there are some who never venture beyond being entry-level Christians (often from lack of good teaching). Walking with God is something separate from, and additional to, the salvation experience. It begins with that one monumental decision, but it doesn't end there. It is a lifetime of day by day, and sometimes minute by minute, choices!

This next section is not intended to be a laundry list of Christian "hoops" which you must immediately jump through, but is an overview of some of the Biblical elements of a mature Christian walk. The interesting thing about being a true child of God is that we "mature" in reverse! Jesus says that we are to "become as little children" (Matthew 18:3), and that God "hast hid these things from the wise and prudent, and hast revealed them unto babes" (Matthew 11:25). Christians are the "little children" and the "babes."

This means that we must die to pride and domination, and that we must embrace humility. In our personal lives, He becomes bigger and we become smaller. It means that we innocently abandon ourselves to trusting our Father in heaven! The reason that certain Christians have "the joy of the Lord" is that they have received the freedom that comes from understanding that we don't have to carry the weight of the world on our shoulders, and that we only need to be concerned about ONE opinion of us…HIS!

So, let's talk about beginning your Christian walk. You may notice that each of these demonstrations of commitment will involve dying to a little piece of yourself…but stepping out in faith will be quickly rewarded with a palpable sense that all of heaven is cheering you on!

Becoming Born Again

For most of my life, I (disdainfully) presumed that "born again Christian" was an expression coined by "fanatical" Southern Baptists (whom I now love and respect)! You can imagine my shamed surprise the first time I read in the Bible, that Jesus Himself says: "Verily, verily, I say unto thee, except a man be born again, he cannot see the kingdom of God" John 3:3 and " Marvel not that I said unto thee, ye must be born again" (John 3:7). It is an expression not just "coined" by Jesus, but commanded by Him!

Being "born again" means dying to all the nonsense that keeps us focused on everything *but* God. It is starting over… acquiring a new heart, a new conscience, and a new set of priorities. I like the saying: "God asks us to give up something that we can't keep anyway (our carnal life) in exchange for something that we can't buy, and can never lose (eternal life with Him)!" He isn't asking us to *physically* give up our lives (even though He asked His Son to do that for us); He is asking us to give up our lives as we *know* them…the things and people that we idolize…the meaningless, worldly things that our lives revolve *around*…and to put Him first. It doesn't mean you can't still have friends, and family, and jobs and fun…(or that you have to give up golf!). They simply can't continue to be the most important things in your life. Anyone who is truly born again can tell you that they are *not* the same person that they were before they allowed Jesus to transform them, and that they have a sense of joy and peace that can only come from God's continual presence in one's life.

Some people teach that being born again happens simultaneously with salvation. That certainly happens (as, perhaps, it just did with you!), when someone comes to the Lord with a repentant heart and desire to change. The Bible also says that, "If any man be in Christ, he is a new creature" (2 Corinthians 5:17), which, of course, is true.

Many people, however, grab on to salvation like a life preserver or an eternal life insurance policy, without any repentance or desire to change. If they have accepted Jesus as their Savior, then the Holy Spirit comes to reside in them, which certainly does make them "new" and gives them the *ability* to think and behave differently…but it is an ability which has to be exercised! God will continue the good work He has begun in us, but some people put up more resistance than others – to the point that we never see evidence of the

"Fruit of the Spirit" in their lives (see Galatians 5:22).

I personally feel that I was saved long before I was "born again"…long before I was willing to give up certain parts of my nature that I thought were just "me" (obnoxious as they may have been!)…and before I was willing to die to my past, knowing that God had blotted it out and pushed the "delete" button on it! Also, I had repented to God for my sins, but it took me a while of walking in the Word, to understand that repentance doesn't just mean saying "I'm sorry," it also means *turning away from* that behavior or thought system.

You and I will always be a "work in progress." Only one person was able to pull off life in the flesh with perfection, and He was God. But, when He is dwelling inside of us, He urges us to turn the controls of the cockpit over to Him…with His laser vision into the past and into the future, and with His nurturing wisdom of what is not only in our *eternal* best interest, but in our best interest for receiving His blessings in this life. He calls for us to "become as little children"—not childish, but trusting Him with childlike faith (see Matthew 18:3).

Once you have been saved, one of the first things Jesus will do is to give you "conviction" (conscience pangs!) about right and wrong and, possibly, about how you spend your time! You may find yourself stricken with guilt every time you do or say something that is offensive to God. That's your cue to say, "I'm sorry, Father," knowing that you are forgiven – but it is also the Holy Spirit, reminding you to claim certain promises from God's Word, such as "Be strong in the Lord and in the power of His might." "I can do all things through Christ, who strengthens me," and "Submit to God, resist the devil, and he will flee from you."

Christians *should* come to the point of being able to 'Just Say No!' to the same old suggestions of their 'flesh' and of the enemy, unless they are in need of serious deliverance. Maturity comes as God molds you on His potter's wheel. How quickly He transforms you depends on whether or not you are willing to be putty in His hands, and whether or not you are willing to stir up, and draw upon, the spiritual giftings which have been placed inside of you, once you have accepted the Savior.

I'm not trying to suggest that being born again is complicated, because *it's not!* God will meet you where you are. I would merely inform you that it is possible to eliminate some Christian "baby steps" by understanding that we really *do* have some free will to exercise here, rather than just expecting Jesus to wave a magic wand over us! It begins with allowing Him to work His will through us.

The Body of Christ is in serious need of mature Christians these days, as record numbers are coming to Christ in need of leadership, instruction, and godly mentoring. If you would like to be used by God, then be willing for Him to "fast track" you…as we seem to, indeed, be living in the "last days"! The "fast" track *won't* be an "instantaneous" track, because growth experiences require time. God wants us to grow into well-rooted oak trees, not mushrooms which spring up overnight!

(By the way, don't be frightened by the thought of living in the "last days." If it is true, then we are truly the *chosen generation*. Every Christian who has ever gone on to heaven, including the apostles of Jesus, would have given their "eye teeth" to be alive when He returns!)

Thoughts on Witnessing

As we read earlier, Jesus said that to be saved, we must "confess" Him. To me, "confessing Jesus" means willingness to publicly acknowledge *all* of Him: His life, His words, His works, His resurrection, and His place in the Godhead. I'm not suggesting that your present belief is as deep as it will some day become. The Word says, "faith comes by hearing the word of God" (Romans 10:17). God knows that faith is progressive...it comes "line upon line, precept upon precept" (Isaiah 28:13). The Word also says, "Whosoever shall call upon the name of the Lord shall be saved" (Romans 10:13). So, no, you don't have to wait until you think you have "stronger faith" in order to be saved or to bear witness about what Jesus has done in your life.

In case you fear that "confessing Jesus" means that every Christian will be called to preach on street corners, or to convert lost souls in the elevator, perhaps it will comfort you to know that this has not been my experience...even though I am called to evangelism. Would I do so if God so urged me? Absolutely! So far, however, the Holy Spirit has always directed me to those individuals to whom He wants me to witness, and either says, "Tell them," or just gives me an irresistible urge to share. I have found, that as long as I stay tuned to and follow His direction, He will almost always have gone before me, preparing that person's heart.

How do I witness? Both actively and passively! Sometimes, it is as simple as (barely audibly) singing a praise song in public. (I do this often, as I am shopping in a grocery or department store.) Sometimes it is by publicly reading my Bible (in airports and restaurants, or in the doctor's office, for example). Also, while shopping, or traveling, or whenever I find something I have been searching for, such as a special bargain, or receive a pleasant surprise of any kind, I am quick to give credit in the form of an enthusiastic "Thank You, Jesus!"…no matter where I am! [These things were never calculated to be witnessing tools, by the way…they are merely manifestations of my personal joy in the Lord, my love for His Word, and my constant amazement at His involvement in my life. Somewhere along the way, He revealed to me how much it pleases Him and what a good witness my joy is to others, so I would never dream of stopping these practices!]

Sometimes, the Lord calls for me to be bold, such as asking a store clerk or waiter where he goes to church. I never cease to be amazed at the witnessing opportunities that just seem to "present themselves"! The Lord will lead total strangers (especially on airplanes!) to open up about their relationships, or their lack of faith, or their children's problems…and that opens the door for more discussion about God and His Word, and for prayer.

With my family and friends, He tells me just to keep working references about Him, and His Word, and what He has done for me, into my conversations. There have been those whom He has had me plant seeds in and then pull back from for a while, and those whom He has had me "press-in" with…even if they seemed irritated by it. I am always more attentive to being obedient, than to worrying about what someone might think or say…although, I admit that it took a while to get to that place! He also frequently tells me to "stifle!" when I feel like adding my two-cents worth, because there is HIS time and place and purpose for everything.

If your witnessing isn't very well received, then ask the Holy Spirit to sharpen your discernment about it, or to give you more boldness, or even less boldness – just to be in His perfect will. Witnessing is much easier these days, because there is so much hunger worldwide for the things of God and for the Truth. Christian television satellites are beaming the Gospel all over the planet, in fulfillment of the Scripture, which proclaims "this gospel of the kingdom shall be preached in all the world for a witness unto all nations, and then the end shall come" (Matthew 24:14). Total world wide coverage is nearing completion! (TBN alone has dozens of satellites covering the globe!)

You might say, "Well, the gospel certainly is available to everyone in *this* country, so why do I have to witness?" For one thing, because it is the Great Commission of Jesus, but also for the same reason that I am writing this book…because there is so much confusion and perversion of the truth, and so many lost generations who have never been exposed to God's "rule book."

Why is there so much ignorance about the Word of God? Because of ancestors who have never been exposed to it, or who have chosen to ignore it or who have "dropped the ball" in passing down God's truths…or who have been too timid or intimidated to share their Christian experience.

Remember Jesus' words: "Whosoever therefore shall be

ashamed of Me and of My words, in this adulterous and sinful generation; of him also shall the Son of Man be ashamed, when He comes in the glory of His Father with the holy angels" (Mark 8:38).

If you are like me, you have cousins and nieces and nephews or children and sisters and brothers who have never received a meaningful explanation (much less a personal testimony) about how and why knowing Jesus can transform one's life, and about why it is the only way to be *certain* of where one will spend eternity. This is not about trying to convince someone that you are right and they are wrong…it is about loving them enough to ask God to use you and to provide opportunities for you (and other laborers) to speak truths into their lives which will transform their eternal destiny!

Thoughts on Water Baptism

If you're serious about wanting to be born again, I would also suggest that you consider being water-baptized (yes, dunked!). Before Jesus began His ministry, John the Baptist prepared the way for Him by calling people to repent and to be baptized in the Jordan River. As soon as Jesus presented Himself to John for water baptism, God spoke from heaven, "This is My beloved Son, in whom I am well pleased" (Matthew 3:16-17). This event also ushered in the beginning of Jesus' ministry…and not by coincidence.

Water baptism represents dying (submersion) and being born anew (arising out of the water), leaving behind all that is past. I believe that if it was important to Jesus and the Father, it should be important to us!

You probably don't have to be submerged to be saved and born again, but I know that it confers a blessing in the spiritual realm which I wouldn't want to be without! (I say "probably," because all He mentioned in Mark 16:15 was that we need to be baptized…but that meant only one thing in His day. If it is available to you, you will feel far more "complete" and "renewed" as a Christian by doing it.)

God really dealt with *me* about putting it off for so long. He finally said to me one day, "If you're waiting for *Me* to create the perfect time for you to get dressed for church, change out of those clothes, put on a robe, and climb into a tank of water, ruining your hairdo, in front of hundreds of people…then you'll never be properly baptized. I'm waiting for *you* to *choose* to follow My leading on this issue!"

I had been waiting for "the magic wand" again (such as an irresistible urging to walk up to the baptismal pool) instead of taking personal responsibility for being in God's will. Needless to say, I was water baptized the next Sunday!

Thoughts on Church Attendance

God says in His Word : "Let us not give up meeting together, as some are in the habit of doing, but let us encourage one another—and all the more as you see the Day approaching" (Hebrews 10:25 NIV).

This is true now more than ever! So, please ask the Lord to guide you to a church that will, ultimately, be an extension of your family. It may take visiting several (more than once) to be certain, but it will be worth the effort.

Above all, look for a pastor who has an anointing to teach the Word of God—not just messages with a moral, based on Christian principles. Anointed teaching will bypass your mind and be deposited straight into your spirit!

Also, look for the presence of the Holy Spirit, whether or not the church claims to be "Spirit-filled." If you ever experience the presence of God in church, you will never forget it, so keep looking until you find it on a regular basis, and then stay there! The anointing for teaching on the ministry of Southern Baptist Pastor Adrian Rogers is as powerful as it is on teacher/evangelist Benny Hinn. So don't assume you can tell by the church "label." (And, I was first taught that by Benny Hinn!)

One reason that sitting under anointed teaching is so important, is that the anointing is "caught," not "taught." If you serve an anointed ministry, that anointing will rub off on your life...it is demonstrated throughout the Old and New Testaments, from accounts of Elijah and Elisha to Jesus and His disciples.

If you, for example, sense the slightest bit of anointing in this manuscript, I can assure you that it's not because I'm anything special, but because I travel for and serve a profoundly anointed ministry, and I have received (and stirred up) an ever-increasing anointing from that service to be used for further service. (The anointing is never for our own personal enjoyment, but to be used for service to others!) I feel certain that I would have never written these words – nor even heard God's directing me to do so – absent having served this anointing. I also belong to and serve an awesome local church, where the presence of God is always palpable and powerful!

You can have a similar experience with the anointing in your local church, if you have an anointed pastor, whom you serve faithfully, simply out of love for God…not out of trying to prove your worth. It may require willingness to do a thankless job, but, as I learned from experience and from good teaching, if you are faithful with the little things that God has given you, He will give you more.

The anointing of some "spiritual mentor" aside, if you want to feel loved and accepted in your church, then *serve* it! Every Christian has a gifting of his very own for some type of service. Let God use you in whatever way He will, rather than waiting for someone to reach out to you. I assure you, they (your church and its members) need you as badly as you need them! As you walk patiently in your anointing, God Himself will eventually promote you to another level.

"Give," (of yourself, your time and your money) "and it shall be given unto you; good measure, pressed down, and shaken together, and running over, shall men give into your bosom. For with the same measure that ye mete withal it shall be measured to you again" (Luke 6:38).

Thoughts on Reading your Bible

If you have been looking up the suggested Scriptures referenced in this reading, then perhaps you are already sensing in your spirit that "this Bible is more than just a book!"

The Bible is the main vehicle that God uses to impart to us revelation about His nature, His will, and His purposes. If you want to feel close to God, it can only happen through studying His Word with a heart that is open to being taught by the Holy Spirit. It has become evident to me that God expects us to know the totality of His Word. Every sentence can't repeat the context of every other preceding sentence, so they are mutually *inclusive*...but God is very patient with us, during the learning process!

Anyone can read the Bible for information. I dare say that the universities of America (and, sadly, some Christian radio airwaves!) are filled with theology instructors who have a head-knowledge about every word of Scripture — yet have no true sense of it (and no true relationship with God), because they don't read it seeking *Him*. I can honestly tell you that I would trash and burn every morsel of education I have ever received (which includes a law degree) in exchange for the knowledge which I have received from seeking God through His Word. It makes everything else I have ever done – not merely pale – but meaningless by comparison!

God says it a hundred times over in Scripture: we are to revere His Word. With this in mind, here is one passage to seriously meditate on ("meditate" meaning: to think about it over, and over again):

"My son, attend to my words, incline thine ear unto my sayings. Let them not depart from thine eyes; keep them in the midst of thine heart. For they are life to those who find them, and health to all their flesh" (Proverbs 4:20-22).

If you will commit that one verse to memory and be obedient to it, it will change your life in a profound way! Then proceed to ask God to show you the verses that would be helpful, in specific situations in your life, and commit them to your memory and to your heart. Perhaps reading a book of "God's Promises" would be one place to start.

Please consider getting your hands on all of the anointed teaching you can…from being in church, watching Christian television, listening to teaching tapes, and/or attending Bible studies, or Bible School…plus your own daily independent Bible study, as guided by the Holy Spirit. (You may think, right now, that this sounds like "Bible overkill," but if God wants to use you, He will put a hunger in you for more of His Word!) No matter how many times you read the Bible, it will speak new revelations to you every time, because it truly *is* the *living Word*! (realize: This is being taught to you by someone who spent most of her life shunning reading the Bible, feeling certain that it would be "too narrow-minded"…while studying every other belief system known to man!)

Speak the Word of God, believing it! Speak it to your situations, to your emotions, to your sick body, to your loved ones, and (especially) to the devil…and watch God work through it in your life!

> "So shall My word be that goes forth out of My mouth: it shall not return unto Me void, but it shall accomplish that which I please, and it shall prosper in the thing whereto I sent it" (Isaiah 55:10,11)

> "Heaven and earth will pass away, but My words will never pass away" (Matthew 24:35 NIV)

> "Let God be found true, though every man be found a liar" (Romans 3:4)

Thoughts on Holy Communion

Jesus obviously understood the significance which the impending shedding of His divine blood was to have on the world and on the Church. Otherwise, He wouldn't have instructed His disciples at

120

the Last Supper to "Do this in remembrance of Me" (Luke 22:19). It is an awesome thing, 2000 years later, that we are still able to draw near to the Lord's table and commune with Him!

We are cautioned by the Apostle Paul in 1 Corinthians 11, never to take communion in a casual or irreverent manner, without discerning (being aware of) the Lord's body. This means that everyone who comes to the Lord's table must be a true believer. Yes, we must repent for our sins as we partake of the sacraments, but we must also be "in remembrance" of the **meaning** of His suffering and sacrifice. Not merely thinking, "Forgive me, Lord, for my sins," but also appreciating that His blood was specifically shed for the remission of our sins, and that His body was beaten so that ours might be healed. ("By whose stripes ye were healed" 1 Peter 2:24 and Isaiah 53:5).

The fact that this verse is found both in the Old and New Testaments signifies that it was a fulfillment of prophecy. In other words, the crucifixion wasn't something that just "happened" to Jesus, it was the **reason** that He came! That portion of Isaiah describes the Messiah:

> "He is despised and rejected of men, a man of sorrows, and acquainted with grief: and we hid as it were our faces from him; he was despised, and we esteemed him not. Surely he hath borne our griefs, and carried our sorrows: yet we did esteem him stricken, smitten of God, and afflicted. But he was wounded for our transgressions, he was bruised for our iniquities: the chastisement of our peace was upon him; and with his stripes we are healed."

When we stop to realize that this was God's long-range plan, brought to fruition, it all makes sense! The work of the Cross is **completed**. Jesus isn't going to climb back up on it and die for us again every time we need forgiveness and healing. Christ died once for all. It is a guarantee, a sure thing, that as soon as we sincerely repent, our sins are already forgiven! It is retroactive! Receive your forgiveness by faith, just as you have received your salvation by faith!

Healing, which is also received by faith, has also already been arranged for us in the heavenlies, because of the work of the Cross. It seems to be more difficult for some to believe in this modern age, but God *is* still in the business of healing. Sometimes it is manifested through miracles, sometimes through progressive healing, sometimes through medical or nutritional channels...but we must examine ourselves, believe the promise, and keep our eyes on the Healer. One excellent book on this subject is *Christ the Healer* by F.F. Bosworth, written in 1877.

Jesus instructed us that as often as we partake of the bread and wine, symbolic of His body and blood, that we are to REMEMBER:

> "And as they were eating, Jesus took bread, and blessed it, and brake it , and gave it to the disciples, and said, Take, eat; this is My body. And He took the cup, and gave thanks, and gave it to them saying, Drink ye all of it: for this is My blood of the new testament, which is shed for many for the remission of sins (Matthew 26:26–28). This is My body which is given for you; this do in remembrance of Me" (Luke 22:19).

Thoughts on the Baptism of the Holy Spirit

There is a Baptism of the Holy Spirit, performed by Jesus, which is separate from and subsequent to, the baptism with water. The receiving of it empowers Christians to become bolder disciples of Christ. Jesus spoke the following truth to His disciples in Acts 1:5: "For John truly baptized with water; but ye shall be Baptized with the Holy Ghost not many days hence." John the Baptist's prophesy of this occurrence is recorded in each of the gospels (Matthew 3:11; Mark 1:8; Luke 3:16; and John 1:33, which states: "The man on whom you see the Spirit come down and remain is He who will baptize with the Holy Spirit. I have seen and I testify that this is the Son of God.")

Many Christians believe that since the Holy Spirit resides in all true believers, that there is no such thing as a separate baptism. This is an understandable perception!

Note, however, that when Jesus appeared to His disciples after the resurrection, He breathed the Holy Spirit into them. "As My Father has sent Me, even so send I you.' And when He had said this, He breathed on them, and saith unto them: 'Receive ye the Holy Ghost.'" This was the imparting of the Holy Spirit to all who believe that He is the resurrected Messiah. All Christians receive it.

Yet, on another instance of appearing to them, He instructed them:

> "And behold I send the promise of my Father upon you; but tarry ye in the city of Jerusalem until ye be endued with power from on high." (Luke 24:49)

123

So, AFTER they had already received the imparting of the Holy Ghost, they were instructed to wait to be "endued" with power (have it put *on* them). The day on which the Holy Spirit showed up, as promised, is called Pentecost, and the 120 people who were waiting "all with one accord in one place," experienced a mighty rushing wind and tongues of fire sitting on each of them. "And they were all filled with the Holy Ghost, and began to speak with other tongues, as the Spirit gave them utterance" (Acts 2:1-4). This was the first Baptism with the Holy Spirit!

Being "filled with the Holy Spirit" doesn't mean that you are more saved or more devout—it just means that you have chosen to take God up on everything He has to offer you. This gift conveys boldness to speak the Word, the ability to receive and understand the Word, and to take authority over the enemy. It also conveys (if one so chooses) the ability to speak in tongues. The gift of tongues allows the Holy Spirit to pray through you, uttering those things which GOD desires to have prayed (Romans 8:26,27).

The Apostle Paul states in 1 Corinthians, that he speaks in tongues more than anyone (14:18), and that he wishes *all* of us would speak in tongues. (Although, he says, it is private communication between one and God, and less educational than prophecy to the rest of the church, unless translated. See 1 Corinthians 14:2-5.) The primary purpose of speaking in tongues; however, is not for the edification of the church—which is why Paul discourages it in that setting. He closes the 14th chapter by encouraging the Corinthians to desire to prophesy, and not to forbid speaking in tongues. He tells the Ephesians to pray "always...in the Spirit" (Ephesians 6:18).

The 120 who were waiting in the Upper Room did not have the gifts of the Spirit dropped upon them unawares. They believed Jesus' promise of His power, desired it, sought it, separated themselves from unbelievers, and obediently waited for 10 days for God's perfect timing to deliver it to them.

If I seem to be matter-of-fact about this experience, it is because I have been a born-again Christian without the baptism of the Holy Spirit – and then *with* it. The difference has been dramatic and life-altering.

Consider this: How will God revive the members of the Body of Christ from being the "silent majority" (who are not united, who never cause any political waves, who rarely tithe or read their Bibles, and seldom if ever reach a lost soul …and who are as sick and depressed and oppressed and as divorced as the non-believing world) into being "the spotless Bride of Christ"? ("That He might present it to Himself a glorious Church, not having spot or wrinkle, or any such thing, but that it should be holy and without blemish" Ephesians 5:2) He will accomplish this by igniting them again with passion and power…and with a desire for holiness, which will bring us full circle to the attributes of the original Church!

The Baptism of the Holy Spirit is available to all true Christians who are leading sanctified lives. God does not fill and empower carnal Christians with His Spirit. If He has put the desire on your heart, then pray that you might receive this spiritual gift, or ask any Spirit-filled Christian to pray with you with the laying on of hands.

Perhaps Oswald Chambers best defines this gift in *My Utmost For His Highest*: "When we receive the Holy Spirit we receive quickening life from the ascended Lord. The Baptism of the Holy Ghost is not an experience apart from Jesus Christ, It is the evidence of the ascended Christ."

Conclusion

Perhaps to some of you the suggestions in this book seem too much like "work"!

Admittedly, there is a dichotomy between the simplicity of being saved (Jesus did *all* the work, all we have to do is believe and receive)—and the seeming "task" of being obedient to God's instructions. Let me assure you that God's grace and patience and love are vast. He is not tapping His foot, saying, "*When* is she going to get this thing *right?*" But, He rejoices when oneness with Him becomes the cry of your heart! That is when He can begin teaching us to rest in Him.

As you walk more closely with the Lord, you begin to take on His nature. The things that are important to God (such as His Son) become equally important to you, and you begin to derive great peace and joy (and protection and provision) from seeking to stay in the center of His will. This doesn't mean that you will never have problems (John 16:33), but once you begin to feel "attached at the hip" to God, there is no fear because He is in the middle of your problem with you. He's bigger than it is, and by faith He will bring you through it in victory (see the entire 91st Psalm; Isaiah 26:3).

The more you rely on Him in times of need, the stronger He will be for you. ("My grace is sufficient for thee, for My strength is made perfect in weakness" 2 Corinthians 12:9.)

I actually argued with God about that Scripture for about a year of my life. "No, Lord, I don't *want* to be weak, just so you can be strong. I want to be strong, too!" Result? He kept bringing me to points of brokenness, where I had nothing to rely on but Him, until I finally gave up the fight, and just said, "Fine, I will trust *You* to take care of it!"—and, He always would! His point was to show me that, if I would "die" to my need to be so self-sufficient, He would be strong, both *for* me, and *through* me. The world might still perceive me as strong and capable, but I have finally come to realize that I *am* nothing, and can *do* nothing, without Him…but by giving Him free reign in my life, in utter *dependence* on His strength and wisdom, there is nothing that I *cannot* do! My job is to be obedient, control my behavior, and allow Him to guide my every step.

All of the positive accomplishments in our lives, which we assume we have performed through our own strength, have actually been performed through His grace. God will allow us to live for just so long under the delusion that we are "self-made men." But, once He draws us nearer and we seek more knowledge of Him, He begins to reveal to us how it really works! This is when profoundly deep faith is birthed – when we see God coming through for us time and time again, simply because we BELIEVE that He will! There are increasing levels of interactions and adventures with God which are activated only by our *surrender.*

We all—man, woman, and child—need to know that we have someone strong to lean on, who is there for us in good times and bad, whom we *trust* to have the *power and the desire* to turn situations around for us...and *who loves us unconditionally!*

The main focus of this writing has been to present *the Truth* and the merits of the gift, which God gave to us in order to demonstrate this love. "For God SO LOVED the world that He gave His only begotten Son, that whosoever believes in Him should not perish, but have everlasting life" (John 3:16). My task was to attempt to broaden your basis of understanding, or perhaps just to plant a seed which someone else might come along and water, so that someday – when your heart is ready – the beauty of it all will blossom forth in you.

May God bless you as you grow into deeper intimacy with Him. May you find His joy and peace manifested in every area of your life and in every cell of your being!

SDG

How to order more copies of Jesus 101

You may order directly from Jesus 101 by mail using a check. Or you may order this book online using a credit card on our secure website at www.Jesus101answers.com or from the publisher, Master Design Ministries, at www.masterdesign.org. You may also call the number below and leave your order and credit card information.

Total Items	Cost	Quantity	Total
1-9 copies	$10 each	_____	_____
10-49 copies	$8 each	_____	_____
50+ copies	$6 each	_____	_____
		Subtotal	_____
	Tennessee residents add 9.25%		_____
	Add shipping and handling cost (see below)		_____
	(Payment must accompany order) **Total**		_____

Shipping & Handling
> For 1ˢᵗ copy: $ 4.00
> For each add'l copy: add $.50 each
> (if over 50 copies, add $.20 for each additional copy)

Name _____

Address (Street) _____

(City, State, Zip) _____

Phone _____

Email (optional) _____

Jesus 101
P. O. Box 38956
Germantown, TN 38183
901-465-7773
www.Jesus101answers.com
Leigh@Jesus101answers.com